Praisow!

'Many companies spend far too much time trying to win approval of their initiatives, and far too little time analysing what the best option is in the first place. In Be Decisive – Now! you will find tools and approaches that might turn your decision-making process on its head . . . in ways which can actually help you make better decisions.'

Bill Schultz, President, Coca-Cola Refreshments Canada

'Want to be a world-class decision maker? Jos van Rozen shows you how with essential tips and rich examples!'

Bill Herbert, Director, Corporate Development, Ruiz Foods

'A comprehensive guide to effective decision making. This book contains a wealth of practical and novel tips that will help bring structure, consistency and increased quality to anyone's decision making.'

Don Fraser, Head of Executive Development, Nokia

'These concepts really work! We implemented many of them in a business process improvement project in 2010. The result was a robust and engaging process that provided timely and effective decisions. The transformation I have seen as a result is truly amazing!'

Richard Sison, MBA, Capex Manager (2007–11),
Coca-Cola Bottlers Philippines, Inc.

'Simple, straightforward, spot-on . . . a practical tool for step-changing organisational decision-making capability.'

Irene Gikemi, Africa Talent Management and
Leadership Development Lead, Bharti Airtel

'The successful make clear decisions and it's personal. Decisions create sovereignty. Decisions put you in control of your domain . . . With this book, you can be sovereign and reign over your domain, through making the right decisions . . . Using any of the ideas in this book just once will earn you back your money.'

David White, Editor In Chief, Who's Who Publications

Be Decisive - Now!

PEARSON

At Pearson, we believe in learning – all kinds of learning for all kinds of people. Whether it's at home, in the classroom or in the workplace, learning is the key to improving our life chances.

That's why we're working with leading authors to bring you the latest thinking and best practices, so you can get better at the things that are important to you. You can learn on the page or on the move, and with content that's always crafted to help you understand quickly and apply what you've learned.

If you want to upgrade your personal skills or accelerate your career, become a more effective leader or more powerful communicator, discover new opportunities or simply find more inspiration, we can help you make progress in your work and life.

Every day our work helps learning flourish, and wherever learning flourishes, so do people.

To learn more, please visit us at **www.pearson.com/uk**

Be Decisive – Now!

The 2-in-1 Manager: Speed Read – instant
tips; Big Picture – lasting results

Jos van Rozen

PEARSON

Harlow, England • London • New York • Boston • San Francisco • Toronto • Sydney
Auckland • Singapore • Hong Kong • Tokyo • Seoul • Taipei • New Delhi
Cape Town • São Paulo • Mexico City • Madrid • Amsterdam • Munich • Paris • Milan

Pearson Education Limited
Edinburgh Gate
Harlow CM20 2JE
United Kingdom
Tel: +44 (0)1279 623623
Web: www.pearson.com/uk

First edition published 2016 (print and electronic)

ISBN: 978-1-292-11977-9 (print)
         978-1-292-11979-3 (PDF)
         978-1-292-11980-9 (ePub)

British Library Cataloguing-in-Publication Data
A catalogue record for the print edition is available from the British Library

Library of Congress Cataloging-in-Publication Data
Names: Rozen, Jos van, author.
Title: Be decisive - now! : the 2-in-1 manager : speed read : instant tips :
   big picture, lasting results / Jos van Rozen.
Description: 1 Edition. | New York : Pearson Education, 2016. | Series: The
   2-in-1 manager
Identifiers: LCCN 2016014345 | ISBN 9781292119779 (pbk.)
Subjects: LCSH: Management.
Classification: LCC HD31 .R786 2016 | DDC 658.4/09—dc23
LC record available at https://lccn.loc.gov/2016014345

10 9 8 7 6 5 4 3 2 1
20 19 18 17 16

Cover design by Two Associates
Print edition typeset in 10/14pt Scene Std by SPi Global
Printed in Great Britain by Henry Ling Ltd, at the Dorset Press, Dorchester, Dorset

NOTE THAT ANY PAGE CROSS REFERENCES REFER TO THE PRINT EDITION

Contents

Contents

About the author

Jos van Rozen is an independent strategy and business case consultant. He works with companies and individuals worldwide to develop compelling business cases for acquisitions, capital projects and major business initiatives.

Originally from the Netherlands, Jos started his working life as a lecturer in Strategic Marketing and Corporate Finance at universities in Helsinki (Finland) and Lincoln (UK). Simultaneously, he marketed Dutch dairy products in Finland for the Campina dairy company.

Following a career change from marketing to finance, Jos joined Georgia-Pacific (soft tissue) and DS Smith Plc (packaging), where he gained over ten years' experience in business modelling, financial analysis and corporate transactions. Over time, he has specialised in the success factors and decision-making process for capital and strategic commitments. His passion is bringing together left- and right-brain thinkers and unleashing the power of their cooperation. Jos's industrial experience covers process industries, packaging, fast-moving consumer goods (FMCG), personal care, soft drinks, business-to-business and office products.

Jos graduated from the Helsinki School of Economics with a business degree in 1995. He lives in London with his family.

For information on his company, please visit www .vanrozenconsulting.com

Acknowledgements

We are grateful to the following for permission to reproduce copyright material:

Photos

Photo on p. 4 © Mazzur/ Shutterstock; photos on pp. 6, 38 (top), 63, 67, 127, 203, 206, 235 (top) and 262 © 123rf.com; photo on p. 10 © windu/ Shutterstock; photo on p. 13 © RAGMA IMAGES/ Shutterstock; photo on p. 18 © DJM-photo/ Shutterstock; photo on p. 20 © Yabresse/ Shutterstock; photo on p. 24 © Kirk Geisler/ Shutterstock; photo on p. 33 © Peshkova/ Shutterstock; photo on p. 34 © holbox/ Shutterstock; photo on p. 35 © Andrew Ward/ Life File/ Photodisc; cartoon on p. 35 and photo on p. 165 © Pearson Education, Inc.; photo on p. 36 © vinzstudio/ Shutterstock; photo (top) on p. 37 © Kriso/ Shutterstock; photos on pp. 37 (bottom) and 149 © iQoncept/ Shutterstock; photo on p. 38 (bottom) © Silberkorn/ Shutterstock; photo on p. 39 © Lissandra Melo/ Shutterstock; photo on p. 57 © Dudarev Mikhail/ Shutterstock; photos on pp. 58 and 132 © Pressmaster/ Shutterstock; photo on p.59 © PanicAttack/ Shutterstock; photo on p. 60 © abimages/ Shutterstock; photo on p. 64 © Sergey Nivens/ Shutterstock; photo on p. 65 (top) © ARTSILENSE/ Shutterstock; photo on p. 65 (bottom) © Vasyl Dudenko/ Shutterstock; photo on p. 66 © Raywoo/ Shutterstock; photo on p. 69 © woaiss/ Shutterstock; photo on p. 71 © gemphoto/ Shutterstock; photo on p. 72 © Dirk Ercken/ Shutterstock; photo on p. 79 © Rob van Haandel (www .mooxx.nl); photo on p. 80 © ktsdesign/ Shutterstock; photo on p. 81 © Tonis Pan/ Shutterstock; photo on p. 82 © Anna Hoychuk/

Acknowledgements

Shutterstock; photo on p.83 (top) © Photodisc; photo on p. 83 (bottom) © Becky Stares/ Shutterstock; photos on pp. 84 and 211 © Kletr/ Shutterstock; photo on p. 85 © Jo Ann Snover/ Shutterstock; photo on p. 121 © Paul Vasarhelyi/ Shutterstock; photo on p. 122 © Everett Collection/ Shutterstock; photo p. 124 © Anna Ewa Bieniek/ Shutterstock; photo on p. 125 © CrackerClips Stock Media/ Shutterstock; photo on p. 126 © gualtiero/ Shutterstock; photo on p. 129 © Kamira/ Shutterstock; photo on p. 138 © Ron Frank/ Shutterstock; photo on p. 141 © Leah-Anne Thompson/ Shutterstock; photo on p. 148 © vladm/ Shutterstock; photo on p. 156 © Gunnar Pippel/ Shutterstock; photo on p. 161 © cloki/ Shutterstock; photo on p. 162 © Stephen VanHorn/ Shutterstock; photo on p. 164 © David Kochermans/ Shutterstock; photo on p. 166 © Greg Epperson/ Shutterstock; ; photo on p. 169 © Jorg Castensen/ Pearson Education, Ltd; photo on p. 181 (top) © Gerasymovych Oleksandr/ Shutterstock; photo on p. 181 (bottom) © melowilo/Shutterstock; photo on p. 182 © efirm/ Shutterstock; photo on p. 188 © PozitivStudija/ Shutterstock; photo on p. 190 © Binski/ Shutterstock; photo on p. 191 © Jcjgphotography/ Shutterstock; photo on p. 195 © mini.fini/ Shutterstock; photo on p. 197 © Microstock Man/ Shutterstock; photo on p. 204 © JohnKwan/ Shutterstock; photo on p. 207 (top) from Robert Elias/ Shutterstock; photo on p.207 (bottom) © robodread/ Shutterstock; photo on p. 208 © hans egbers/ Shutterstock; photo on p. 212 © Dusit/ Shutterstock; photo on p. 221 © auremar/ Shutterstock; photo on p. 225 © Pincasso/ Shutterstock; photo on p. 229 © EdBockStock/ Shutterstock; photo on p. 232 © Valentyn Volkov/ Shutterstock; photo on p. 234 © zimmytws/ Shutterstock; photo on p. 235 (bottom) © Tatiana Popova/ Shutterstock; photo on p. 241 © Sabphoto/ Shutterstock; photo on p. 242 © Ernest R. Prim/ Shutterstock; photo on p. 243 © Johann Helgason/ Shutterstock; photo on p. 244 (top) © Jirsak/ Shutterstock; photo on p. 244 (bottom) © Jeff Thrower/ Shutterstock; photo on p. 245 © Oleksiy Mark/ Shutterstock; photo on p. 246 © John Foxx Collection/ Imagestate; photo on p. 248 © PhotoLiz/ Shutterstock; photo on p. 253 © Mihai Simonia/ Shutterstock; photo on p. 256 © Joanchang/ Shutterstock.

Figures

Figure on p. 123 from The CEO Report, *Embracing the Paradoxes of Leadership and the Power of Doubt,* Heidrick & Struggles, January 2015; table and figure on pp. 184–5 from 'Are you ready to decide?', April 2015, *McKinsey Quarterly,* www.mckinsey.com. Copyright © 2015 McKinsey & company. All rights reserved. Reprinted with permission.

Chapter 1

Get the problem right

1.1 Create distance, set the context first

Many decision processes in business start with a solution rather than a problem. Paint a picture of the business context to help you unveil hidden problems. Simply state the facts and try to connect the dots before even contemplating what the problem may be, if any. For a more inclusive context, include multiple perspectives. Yet, even using a multi-perspective context does not necessarily mean your context is wide enough.

Six blind men and an elephant

There's an old parable from India that illustrates the limits of personal perspectives. The gist of it is that six blind men want to learn what an elephant is like, having never seen one. They are brought to an elephant and each touches a part of the animal, but only that one part (one feels the trunk, another a tusk, another a leg, another the tail, etc). When they report back, they find they completely disagree about what an elephant is. One says it's like a snake, another like a spear, another like a pillar, and so on. The moral of the story is that each of our perspectives is valid, but no one is likely to have a complete picture of the situation. Only by working together, and integrating our perspectives, can we come closer to the truth.

Do this
Run your context analysis by a co-worker and ask them to spot any implied solutions and highlight missing information.

1.2 Sift symptoms from causes

Solving an apparent problem may not address the real issue. Convince yourself that you have drilled down to the root cause.

Use common techniques such as the 5 Whys or a fishbone diagram to achieve this quickly.

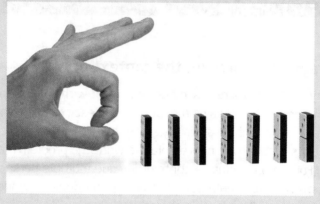

Source: Mazzur/Shutterstock

Do this

When looking for root causes, pay particular attention to indications of broken processes or alterable behaviour.

1.3 Know your strategic priorities

Not every problem needs to be solved right now. Not every problem needs to be solved by your company. Be clear on the strategic priorities: focus on protecting, creating or expanding the organisation's future profit sources. The more explicit these are, the easier it is to keep a cool head and be as clear about your 'NOT to do' list as you are about your 'To do' list.

To do list:
– Focus exclusively
  on strategic
  priorities

NOT to do list:
– Flavour of the month
– Just in case things
– Distractions

Do this

Say 'No' to ideas that are not clearly advancing your game. More focus and time for the things that matter are your reward.

1.4 Articulate your problem statement

Even if a problem is clear to you, others are likely to have a different interpretation. This is where expectations and results start to diverge. Spell it out as clearly and explicitly as you can to prevent misunderstandings.

Do this

Focus on outcomes (= results) rather than outputs (= actions completed).

1.5 Validate your problem with stakeholders

The worst decisions are taken in isolation or with stakeholder involvement too late in the process to make a meaningful difference. Use their insights, worries and questions to craft a better supported problem statement.

Extra benefit: Doing this will also set you up for more involved stakeholder support later in the process, typically allowing for faster decisions.

> *'If people are so bad at making decisions, how did we make it to the moon? The answer is: Individuals didn't make it to the moon; NASA did.'*

(Chip Heath)

Source: 123rf.com

Do this
Seek out dissenting voices. Listen to their concerns. Acknowledge and address their points.

1.6 Filter out problem and solution bias

We are all prone to bias, and it is most difficult to recognise in ourselves. Put a few simple checks in place to recognise and deal with bias. That way you can give every situation a fair chance to be crystallised into the right problem.

Do this
Let a cross-functional group identify the problem for a more inclusive perspective.

1.7 Be clear about ownership and key roles

Every project should have a business owner to ensure benefit delivery. Very often the project implementer is regarded as the project owner. When the project is complete, the project owner typically moves on to the next project. Does that ensure the project delivers its benefits once implementation is complete?

Getting your problem right is crucial to getting the right business owner bought in to it.

Phase:	Idea exploration	Business case & approval	Implementation	Benefit delivery
Typical Ownership:	Project champion		Project manager	Business as usual. . .
Ownership for value delivery:	Business project owner			

Do this

Let a cross-functional group identify the problem for a more inclusive perspective.

Reference

Heath C, Larrick R and Klayman J (1998) Cognitive repairs: How organizational practices can compensate for individual shortcomings. *Research in Organizational Behavior*, 20: 1–37.

1.1 Create distance, set the context first

Why

Working without context is like going on a trip without a map. You don't know where you are, and you are in the dark about where you're going. Without looking at the context, many people overlook the bigger picture, miss opportunities or simply end up working on the wrong problems. The simple act of articulating your view on context forces you to put some facts and observations to paper. This helps you to create distance and add objectivity to the situation you are looking to address.

Getting buy-in for your plans is a lot harder when other stakeholders do not have a clear picture of how those plans impact their own priorities.

Business briefing

McKinsey, the consultancy, has investigated the traits of companies and their decision-making track record. This shows that planning in context matters. Decisions made at companies without any strategic planning process were found to be twice as likely to have generated extremely poor results as extremely good ones.

This excerpt from an interview with Derk Haank, CEO of Springer Nature, shows the importance of taking external factors into account:

> '*I investigated the brick industry at a time of great upheaval. On the one hand were the small, traditional businesses with old ovens that backed a brick every once in a while. On the other hand were the modern businesses with investments in state of the art equipment that were about to go belly-up due*

to their inability to meet interest payments. That would be a pity. The solution was that you paid the traditional businesses a premium in exchange for their promise not to use their ovens anymore.'

Source: windu/Shutterstock

The cost of the premium was not factored in as part of the original investment for the state-of-the-art factories. You could consider it tuition for failing to see that other players viewed the same market in a different way, and for ignoring the impact of interest charges on minimum pricing. Just having the lowest operating cost was not sufficient to get to break-even volumes when there were also interest charges to pay. Paying the premium was still more attractive than the then-prevailing situation.

Try this

Next time you are working on a business case, ask yourself these questions:

- Why am I looking at this situation now?
- What events and trends have led to the current situation?
- Has this happened before?

- What are the business implications of it not being resolved?
- What is the prize for resolving it well?
- What changes in external factors could evaporate or exacerbate the problem?

Tip

You are your own biggest enemy when it comes to painting an objective picture of the context. For a quick, big difference, ask for the input of just one co-worker. Run your context description by them and ask whether they can spot any implied solutions or missing pieces of information.

Reflection

- How did it work?

- What will I do next time?

Reference

'Het blijft lekker als mensen gewoon doen wat je zegt.' ('It stays nice when people just do what you say.') Interview Derk Haank by Jannetje Koelewijn. NRC.nl, 24 October 2015. Translation: Jos van Rozen.

1.2 Sift symptoms from causes

Why

Just as with diseases, taking away the symptom that is causing the inconvenience may not address the underlying illness. Inappropriate treatment will just cause bigger problems further ahead.

Business briefing

The University of Oxford surveyed more than 5,400 large IT projects worldwide. They defined 'large' as having an initial price tag of over $15m. On average, large IT projects run 45 per cent over budget and deliver 56 per cent less value than predicted. In other words, for every three percentage points of projected RoI (Return on Investment) only one gets delivered. Remember that the next time you prepare or review a project for approval!

The survey shows that these results primarily originated from having unclear objectives and shifting requirements. With symptoms being held as problems, you can see how teams struggle to deliver project benefits when they are not addressing the root cause.

Try this

For your next problem definition, use the power of the 5 Whys to sift symptoms from causes. Simply start with what you think the problem is and explain why (note: first Why) the problem has occurred. This answer forms the basis to the next 'Why' question. Keep going like this until you have reached the root cause. This will typically take you up to five Whys. Note that each 'Why' question may have multiple answers. Each needs to be explored with further Whys.

Tips

- You will know that you have reached the root cause when your answer refers to a broken process or alterable behaviour.
- Use a fishbone diagram to allow for your analysis to be branched and provide multiple root causes.

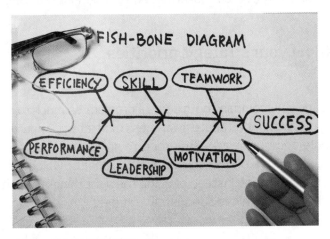

Source: RAGMA IMAGES/Shutterstock

Reflection

- How did it work?

- What will I do next time?

Reference

Bloch M, Blumberg S and Laartz J (2012) *Delivering Large-scale IT Projects on Time, on Budget, and on Value.* McKinsey & Company.

1.3 Know your strategic priorities

Why

You and your company both share a problem: so much to do, so little time. Without an acute awareness of strategic priorities, many people and businesses are prone to spreading themselves too thin. They work on too many projects, most of which are urgent but not important. Instead of doing the right things well, they end up doing many things adequately – at best.

Business briefing

In the management classic *Good to Great*, Jim Collins investigates what long-term successful companies do to continue outperforming their peers. One of his key findings relates to clarity of strategic priorities, combined with an awareness of this among the workforce.

When everyone is working on the same few things that really matter, their actions will be mutually supportive. At the same time, clarity about what matters makes it very easy for any employee to say 'no' to ideas that are a distraction. This means that the screening out of less relevant initiatives can happen anywhere in the organisation and is not the exclusive preserve of top management. This 'self-screening' eliminates uncountable hours spent crafting business cases and gaining support for projects that are not right for your organisation. This is time that you can use instead to focus on value delivery for your priority projects. How valuable is that?

Try this

- Get your hands on the current set of strategic priorities for your organisation.
- Create your own list if no documented set of priorities exists. This should identify the two or three main sources of future profit for the business.
- Confirm that the strategic priorities focus on (1) protecting, (2) creating or (3) expanding the organisation's future profit sources.
- Verify for chosen opportunities that you have a Right to Succeed[1] in delivering the desired outcome.
- Reject any ideas that distract from working on the strategic priorities as early as possible. Be clear to the initiator about the reasons for rejection.

Tip

Refer regularly to your strategic priorities. Screen your own activities against them and mention them in your interactions with others. This promotes a shared understanding of priorities and aligned activities.

---

[1] Right to Succeed: the factors that entitle you to be successful at delivering the outcome(s). This can include a wide range from available skills and prior track record to market position and intellectual property.

Reflection

- How did it work?

  ```



  ```

- What will I do next time?

  ```



  ```

Reference

Collins J (2001) *Good to Great: Why Some Companies Make the Leap . . . and Others Don't*. Random House.

1.4 Articulate your problem statement

'A problem well-stated is a problem half-solved.'

(Charles Kettering, serial inventor[2])

Why

The quality of our solutions stands in direct proportion to the quality of the problems we are trying to solve. Spelling out your

---

[2] Charles Kettering is known for inventing, among many other things, the electrical starting motor, leaded gasoline, the refrigerant Freon and the world's first aerial missile.

problem forces you to think about its causes, its importance and links to other aspects of the business. This gives you a chance to solidify your logic, challenge your assumptions and create a platform for generating potential solutions.

'If I were given one hour to save the planet, I would spend 59 minutes defining the problem and one minute resolving it.'

(Albert Einstein)

Business briefing

A problem statement is a description of a situation that needs to be resolved. It can also be described as either a gap between the current and the desired state or a contradiction between principle and practice. The ultimate goal of a problem statement is to transform a generalised problem into a targeted, well-defined problem that can be resolved.

The pitfalls surrounding problem statements are typically:

- They are too general. This allows for multiple interpretations and causes misalignment.
- They are too specific, ignoring the bigger picture.
- The solution is 'baked' into the problem statement. The purpose of the problem statement is to find the best solution. If the solution is already cast by the problem statement, you are missing out on other ideas.

Try this

For your next problem statement, do this:

- Be fact based. State what has happened or is happening and how this impacts the business.
- Be general enough to allow for a range of alternative solutions to be considered.
- Be specific enough to allow for a focused effort on finding solutions.

▶

- If addressing an opportunity, use directional terms rather than definitive numbers; for example, 'we can grow our volume' vs 'we can grow our volume by 10 per cent'. The latter implies that you already know how [solution!] you are going to grow your volume. You can only know the magnitude of the change once you know the solution, and we're not talking about solutions just yet.

Tip

Use the other side of the proverbial coin and word your problem instead as an opportunity. This can generate some creative ideas to 'regular' problems.

Source: DJM-photo/Shutterstock

Reflection

- How did it work?

- What will I do next time?

1.5 Validate your problem with stakeholders

Why

Decisions initiated and approved by the same person generate the worst financial results. Where stakeholders are involved, this often happens too late in the process to make a meaningful difference. By the time they get to voice their concerns, they are typically perceived as slowing the approval process down, rather than contributing to a better decision.

Once a problem statement has been cast in stone, it is natural for most people to take it as a given. Yet, it is getting others involved at this stage that increases their interest in the project. Early involvement allows them to make a meaningful contribution from the start, to the extent that you may well end up with a different solution, or even a different problem statement altogether. It also gives stakeholders a chance to understand and challenge your ingoing assumptions and scope. The more alignment there is about the problem statement, the more involvement and support you are likely to get from other stakeholders further down the line.

Business briefing

Executives at companies with satisfactory[3] outcomes from strategic business decisions rate their processes highly when

---

[3] Satisfactory is here defined modestly as 'meets or exceeds expectations'. Although the term is somewhat downbeat, it makes sense when you realise that the *average* business decision generates only about a third of the intended return. In other words, 'meeting expectations' is already pretty good.

it comes to seeking contrary evidence. Where results meet or exceed expectations, companies report in roughly two thirds of cases that they encourage robust discussions. For projects with unsatisfactory results, this is only the case 37 per cent of the time, underscoring the value of good discussion.

Here are some of the practices successful companies deploy:

- Ensure that decision makers have all the critical information.
- Give dissenting voices the floor.
- Review the business case thoroughly, even though senior executives may be strongly in favour.
- Ensure that truly innovative ideas reach senior managers.

Source: Yabresse/Shutterstock

Try this

- Involve your stakeholders right from the start. Their perspective can help you see the problem from different angles. This will give you a useful sense for key issues and alignment enablers.
- Keep the process light. A 15-minute brainstorm session already goes a long way in identifying any sticking points. Before you close the session, clarify the questions that *must* be answered to enable you to solidify the problem statement.

Tips

- Keep an open mind about who your relevant stakeholders are. This group may evolve over time. Ask your identified stakeholders who they think should be involved, or let any unanswered questions drive this.

- Companies with many projects running concurrently address the early stakeholder challenge by having a project portfolio management system. Whenever a new project is initiated, all heads of department receive an alert. They must then indicate: (a) whether they support the project being initiated and (b) whether they need to be involved in key project decisions.

  A perfect way to create early awareness and buy-in at senior level!

- If there are no obvious other stakeholders to your project, do ask for input from other sources on your problem statement anyway. It's a great way to hold up a figurative mirror and improve your thinking.

- For my own business cases, I use my rule of thumb[4] that every additional perspective will increase the quality of the problem statement by its inverse fraction. That's a sophisticated way of saying what the graph below attempts to show.

Problem definitions get better with more stakeholder perspectives

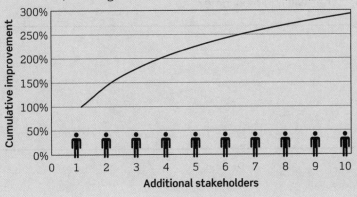

Additional stakeholders

---

[4] No empirical science here, just a guide to remind myself of something I have found very valuable over time: to include multiple perspectives.

This means that by just asking one person for input you should expect to roughly double the quality of what you are working on. Asking another three will add the same amount of value. From around the 6–7-mark you will find the extra value starts to level off. Beware that this is only a guide. If the first seven people you ask all pay lip-service to what they perceive to be your intentions, then their added value will undoubtedly be less. Remember what successful companies do: seek out alternative views to strengthen the case.

Reflection

- How did it work?

- What will I do next time?

Reference

McKinsey & Co (2009) Flaws in strategic decision making. *McKinsey Quarterly*, January 2009.

1.6 Filter out problem and solution bias

Why

The results of the average business decision fall short of original expectations. The explanation is often related to unforeseen circumstances. These, in turn, are largely explained by bias, as bias filters how we look at our world and what we take into account for our decisions. This is either bias not to think wide enough about a problem's context, or simply bias towards a solution. The latter is often combined with 'reverse-engineering' a problem to suit that solution.

Business briefing

A lack of context gives way to problem bias. This is one of the biggest culprits of the corporate world's poor decision-making track record. You have made up your mind about what the problem is, and that's it. With a shared, more objective understanding of context you vastly reduce the occurrence of problem bias.

Bias /'bʌɪəs/ noun *inclination or prejudice for or against someone or something, especially in a way considered to be unfair.*

McKinsey also reports that when it comes to business decision making, the basic assumption of modern economics – rationality – does not stack up against the evidence. Instead, many decisions are driven by politics, solution bias and a partial fact base. In other words, people tend to work with the facts that suit their story rather than 'the truth, the whole truth and nothing but the truth'.

Example

Yellowstone National Park is a vast area in the US state of Wyoming, and the natural habitat of rattle snakes, bison, grey wolves and elk. Between 1994 and 2014, the elk population fell from tens of thousands of elk to just a few thousand. Local inhabitants have been quick to point out the role of the controversial reintroduction of the grey wolf into Yellowstone. Researcher Arthur Middleton studied the Yellowstone elk for five years to conclude that there is a multitude of factors contributing to the elk population's decline, of which reintroduced predators such as grey wolves actually have a relatively small impact.

Source: Kirk Geisler/Shutterstock

Without proper context and fact-finding, it would have been easy to give way to local residents' demands to address the grey wolves' presence in the park as a way to stop the elk population's decline. Middleton concluded that this would have been an insignificant solution to address the decline.

Try this

Emotional engagement and industry experience are serious contributors to the occurrence of bias. At a high level, the answer then is to keep as much emotional distance as possible. In practice, this is difficult for most people to do naturally. To overcome this, work with check lists or a fishbone diagram.[5] This helps to assure that every situation is treated the same way, and that you can check back on that. Alternatively, look at your situation through the eyes of an outsider. Identify what they would first ask or say about your problem statement.

Example

In 1985 Intel found itself at a major crossroads. The company was involved in developing and manufacturing memory chips and microprocessors. The company had grown on the back of memory chips, a market where Japanese competitors were beating American players on both cost and quality. The market for microprocessors was relatively undeveloped, but looked promising.

Intel did not have the resources to play in both markets and a debate was dividing the company about which horse to back. Many long-time Intel managers favoured to stay with what they knew best [note: bias]: memory chips. Andy Grove and Gordon Moore, Intel's leaders at the time, found themselves in

▶

5 Fishbone diagrams are causal diagrams created by Kaoru Ishikawa (1968) and show the causes of a specific event. Common uses of the fishbone diagram are product design and quality defect prevention, to identify potential factors causing an overall effect. Each cause or reason for imperfection is a source of variation. Causes are usually grouped into major categories to identify these sources of variation. It is known as a fishbone diagram because of its shape, similar to the side view of a fish skeleton.

a conundrum, not sure what to do. That is, until one day Grove asked Moore this question:

- 'What would happen if somebody took us over and got rid of us – what would the new guy do?' he said.
- 'Get out of the memory business,' Moore answered.

Grove agreed. And he suggested that *they* be the ones to get Intel out of the memory business. This simple shift of perspective helped them to gain the mental distance necessary for a more objective approach and move on.

Tips

- There are many different forms of bias. If you want to check yourself and your co-workers for bias, read Section 2.6. Simply being aware of bias is an important first step in avoiding it.
- Focus on *outcomes* (results) instead of *outputs* (tasks completed) to avoid solution bias.
- Be mindful of who is involved in defining the problem; if you hand a situation to an engineer, you'll get an engineering problem and a solution to match. The same applies to other departments. Where possible, cast your net wider and involve multiple departments, even if just for one short session.

Reflection

- How did it work?

- What will I do next time?

References

Ishikawa K (1989) *Introduction to Quality Control.* JUSE Press Ltd.

Roxburgh C (2003) Hidden flaws in strategy. *McKinsey Quarterly,* 2: 27–40.

Wilcox C (2014) Why are Yellowstone's elk disappearing? *Discover* magazine, 18 April 2014.

1.7 Be clear about ownership and key roles

Why

There are two distinct points to be made about ownership. They relate to ownership of project implementation and ownership of value delivery. A project's implementer needs to be involved in the decision-making process, ideally from as early on as possible. This gives you a free and highly valuable reality check on deliverability and required resources, and immediately boosts your chances of success and engagement when it comes to meeting expectations.

The second point is about overall project ownership. This is ownership for delivering the profit and loss (P&L) benefits of the decision, and would typically be an operational role. He/she needs to be driving the project forward in a hands-on way. The project owner must want to know how the project comes together, what its critical elements are and how value delivery is being assured. Without this clarity of ownership, a project simply increases its chances to flounder.

Business briefing

There is a reason private equity businesses are comparatively successful. A lot is explained by clarity of ownership. When people know the 'buck stops with them', they will pull out all the stops to make sure no stone is left unturned to make the venture a success. This builds on Jim Collins' point made under 'Know your strategic priorities': great[6] companies know to create awareness in their employees of where the business is going and the distinct role their employees play in getting there. When your expected contribution is clear, embracing ownership is a lot easier.

Try this

- Just use this simple rule: Beyond initial exploration, projects should *only* be resourced when a project owner is in place. It is crucial that the project owner has a vested operational interest in addressing the problem you have identified.
- Create and sustain the awareness in the project team about the business results it is aiming to achieve.

Tip

For any decision you work on, assure yourself that there is a clearly identified business owner driving the decision. Raising this question will help crystallise the urgency and desirability of the decision for the business. Contrast this to a solution sponsored by a support department without a demand-driven business need.

---

[6] 'Greatness' is defined here as financial performance several multiples better than the market average over a sustained period.

Reflection

- How did it work?

- What will I do next time?

Chapter 2

Develop creative alternatives

2.1 Alternatives are more than contrasting props

Alternative solutions are often abused to make the favoured solution look desirable. The bigger the contrast, the more obvious the case for that solution becomes. This is a careless game. It also ignores the value alternatives can bring to the ultimately recommended solution. Be serious about getting the best ideas on the table. After all, you cannot discard an idea that you haven't considered.

Source: Peshkova/Shutterstock

'In order for the light to shine so brightly, the darkness must be present.'

(Sir Francis Bacon)

Do this
Aim to generate at least two alternative solutions that solve the problem by using different resources.

2.2 Go for unique ideas to bolster your competitive position

Most business projects are marginal improvements or updates of existing concepts. Focus on unique ideas to give yourself a better chance to stand out from the competition.

Source: holbox/Shutterstock

Do this

Set your mind to *solve a problem* rather than to *justify* a solution.

2.3 Think outside the box!

You probably thought that creative ideas are for that rare breed of blue-sky thinkers. Think again. Just take a moment to identify what you see as your situation's constraining factors. Simply question those to get new insights.

Source: Andrew Ward/Life File/Photodisc

Do this

Look at your problem definition and screen it for potentially limiting factors. To what extent are the conditions for a solution already baked in to the problem statement? Could a different way of phrasing open the door to a wider array of solutions?

2.4 Focus on bigger problems to find bigger solutions

The solutions to bigger problems typically address problems of a smaller scale or scope just as well. It does not necessarily work the other way round.

Source: Pearson Education, Inc.

'Give a man a fish, and you feed him for a day; teach him how to catch fish, and you feed him for a lifetime.'

(Attributed to Anne Isabella Thackeray
Ritchie's (1837–1919) novel, *Mrs. Dymond*)

Do this

Multiply the metrics of your problem by a factor ten. Do your original solutions still fit the bill? What new solutions can you think of?

2.5 Use clear ground rules for productive brainstorming

Great ideas are not born in silos. Cross-functional brainstorming can be very quick, efficient and powerful. With some clear ground rules, participants can get more out of a brainstorm session.

Source: vinzstudio/Shutterstock

Do this

Clarify the real criteria the company uses for decision making. Ask targeted questions that take people out of their existing mental boxes. Select participants who can answer the questions you are asking.

2.6 Give your alternatives an honest, fair chance

You have gone through a lot of trouble to get some unique ideas on the table. Don't spoil it by falling foul of the contrasting fallacy and other biases. Set clear evaluation criteria for screening.

Source: Kriso/Shutterstock

'We forget the chains we wear in life.'

(Charles Dickens)

Do this

Task someone with a 'devil's advocate' role. Let them challenge both the problem and the merits of the proposed solution(s).

Source: iQoncept/Shutterstock

2.7 Go on, do cherry pick

The word 'alternative' itself implies that you choose either the one or the other. Step out of this box and break the myth of mutual exclusivity. Pick the best bits from each idea and amalgamate them into a super-charged recommendation.

Do this

When generating alternatives, specifically look at 'low-cost' and 'no-cost' solutions. These tend to be very suitable for parallel implementation, and may spark some ideas that can be bolted on to more resource-intensive solutions.

Source: 123rf.com

Source: Silberkorn/Shutterstock

From OR-OR thinking . . .

Source: Lissandra Melo/Shutterstock

. . . to AND-AND thinking.

2.1 Alternatives are more than contrasting props

Why

Alternatives are tremendously useful. That's why most organisations require an evaluation of alternatives in their business cases for initiatives. Unfortunately, their utility is often degraded to merely help justify the choosing of a favoured solution rather than making full use of the benefits that alternatives offer.

In a way this is understandable. Most projects start with a solution re-engineered into a problem. There is typically little time for extensive exploration of other alternatives and doing so almost seems absurd when there is a perfectly viable alternative ready to be served up. From that perspective, the alternatives section of the business case becomes a box-ticking exercise; some other potential solutions have to be included to demonstrate a form of due diligence was applied when settling for the recommended solution. But consider this: you can never discard an alternative that you haven't considered. The richer your range of choice, the richer your potential pickings.[1]

Business briefing

Note: In everyday parlance, 'alternatives' is often used interchangeably with 'options'. For the purpose of excellence in decision making, I hope we can agree to just refer to 'alternatives' when it comes to talking about potential solutions. That way, we can reserve 'options' as our term for a risk management tool.[2]

---

[1] Caveat: more is not always better. For some problems there are simply less good solutions than others. You'd then rather be looking at two good alternatives than four mediocre ones.

[2] See Chapter 6.

In their book *Decisive*, Chip and Dan Heath refer to two insightful studies when it comes to the value of alternatives in successful decision making. Firstly, most organisations, whether profit, non-profit or public sector, are ignorant of the choices they have. Seventy per cent of organisations approach their problems not unlike teenagers, where the dominant thinking pattern is one of 'Should I do this or not?' rather than 'What should I do (about this)?' From a successful decision-making perspective, looking at multiple alternatives adds noticeable value compared to 'whether or not' decisions. One study into the decision track record of a private, mid-sized technology firm in Germany revealed that decisions are six (!) times more likely to turn out really well when two alternatives are considered, compared to 'whether or not' decisions. If we just define 'really well' as 'meeting or exceeding expectations', imagine what a big jump in project returns we could achieve from the current reality shown by the University of Oxford study in Section 1.2.

In other words: alternatives have real value-accretive potential.

Try this

Ask yourself these questions:

- Are my alternatives *real* alternatives or just variations of a favoured solution?

Look at a wide set of alternatives:

- What would low-cost solutions look like?
- Are there alternatives that solve defined parts of the problem?
- What would wider scope solutions look like?
- Does the problem definition implicitly impose restrictions?

Review the list of alternatives. Does that spark any further ideas?

Tips

- A great shortcut to creative results in this area is to think 'and' instead of 'or'.
- Ultimately, the value generated by the review of alternatives stands or falls with the amount of genuine effort that went into putting a range of creative alternatives together – mind you, putting that together is often easier than people think. Just give it your best, knowing that even just one more alternative can already make a big difference.

Reflection

- How did it work?

- What will I do next time?

References

Gemünden HG and Hauschildt J (1985) Number of alternatives and efficiency in different types of top-management decisions. *European Journal of Operational Research*, 22: 178–190.

Heath C and Heath D (2013) *Decisive: How to Make Better Choices in Life and Work*. Random House.

Nutt PC (1993) The identification of solution ideas during organizational decision making. *Management Science*, 39: 1071–1085.

2.2 Go for unique ideas to bolster your competitive position

Why

Most business projects are marginal improvements or updates of existing concepts. Marginal projects typically generate marginal benefits. The businesses that stand out do so because of a unique idea. This can be a unique product, a unique way of producing it or a unique way of delivering it or its benefits. By focusing on generating unique ideas you give yourself a better chance to carve out your own space in the market place.

Business briefing

Problem solving vs solution justification

Most projects start with an answer already in mind. A lot of the work done focuses on justifying the project to be approved. Against a background of good intentions and decent returns, stakeholders are on the face of it not unreasonable in their conclusion that they must be looking at the right answer.

> 'The odds of finding a unique answer go way up if you are actually looking for it.'
>
> (Bill Schultz, President, Coca-Cola Refreshments Canada)

However, the power of looking for alternatives comes from two distinct prongs. Firstly, the more you look for alternatives, the more you might come up with a better answer. I say *might*, because there is a caveat to this that we will address shortly. The second prong is the more important one: where you change your effort from justifying the solution to truly solving the problem at hand, this changes the discussion, and potentially the individuals involved.

How you define the problem drives your range of alternatives

Typically when switching focus from justifying the solution to solving the problem, the scope gets wider. This opens up a new realm of potential solutions, underscoring the point that your range of alternatives will be driven by how you define the problem.

Example

A packaged foods business sells products in tins. As the filling line for tins runs out of capacity, the plant manager responsible for assuring sufficient supply proposes a project that expands the tin-filling production capacity. Taking this slightly wider, the procurement manager suggests considering outsourcing some of the tin-filling capacity to avoid having to make the investment.

Hearing about this, the product manager realises that the sales volume has been pushed aggressively with a low-price strategy and that a switch to a more premium price approach may slow down volume growth and yet generate more profit (potentially avoiding the higher costs of outsourcing or the need for investment). If that wasn't enough, the group marketing manager, responsible for the performance of a portfolio of products and packaging types, then shares the insight that there's still plenty of filling capacity for other packaging formats (glass jars, pouches, cartons), with some formats offering more user convenience than tins.

Relentless effort

Earlier in this chapter we made the point that the more you look for alternatives, the more likely you are to come up with a better answer. A cynic might counter that by asking 'What if you came up with the best answer first?'

From the workshops I have run over the years, I can report that this rarely happens. And for a good reason. Whenever we challenge the participants with a brain teaser for which they need to find a solution, there's typically a sigh of relief when a solution has been found. The body language changes: people start to lean back.

'Competition begins where we stop looking!'

(Bill Schultz)

When they are then encouraged to dig deeper to find more solutions, they go back to work. And, interestingly, they keep finding things. Even more interestingly, the most elegant solutions come at the end. And most of the time, in retrospect, people cannot imagine having come up with the more elegant solution earlier in the process. They have gone from a somewhat hard-to-achieve solution to something seemingly impossible. In other words, most of the time, this is a journey of progression where perseverance pays off. Often, the person with the best solution is the one who will win.[3]

And – relying on the pattern-recognition bias here[4] – history has born this out. Spread sheets were not invented by Microsoft, they just made them better. Hamburgers were not invented by McDonald's, they just found a smart way to sell billions of them.[5] Sam Walton didn't invent self-service discount stores, he was just passionate about learning from others and applying that insight with zeal in his Walmart stores.

Connect to competitive position

In his classic *Competitive Advantage,* Michael Porter outlines the importance of differentiation, cost leadership and focus strategies to secure a competitive advantage. Essentially a

---

[3] Note here that the market will ultimately be the judge of what is 'best'. This is witnessed by the 1980s video tape format war, where the technologically deemed superior Betamax format lost out to VHS, driven by cost and recording time being key factors for consumers' purchasing decisions.

[4] See Section 2.6.

[5] McDonald's stopped counting the number of hamburgers sold in April 1994, when the number had passed 99 billion.

competitive advantage answers the question, 'Why should the customer purchase from this operation rather than the competition?'

Where historically many businesses were driven over time to compete on price (and thus cost) as their business commoditised, this has changed with the growth of differentiation and niche strategies. Even in highly commoditised markets such as agriculture or mining it is possible to command market premiums through differentiation based on service, quality or innovation. A great example of this is the innovation of baby carrots, cut from previously discarded off-specification carrot shapes, turning waste from a cost item into a highly profitable revenue stream.

'If you don't have a competitive advantage, don't compete.'
Jack Welch, former Chairman and CEO, General Electric

Considering competitive advantage when it comes to alternatives ensures that any alternative does not just address a problem, but also maintains or improves the company's competitive position. In other words, a good project is not good enough – the litmus test is to craft *winning solutions* for the market place.

Example

Businesses frequently spend millions of pounds to 'guarantee' that they will lose to the competition in the market every day – for years!

The graph below shows company A considering an investment to lower its cost structure by 15 per cent. Although this may appear an impressive leap ahead, this merely contributes to an extension of misery if the competition already has a 45 per cent cost advantage. Once the investment has been made, the company will be 'stuck' with that solution for the foreseeable future while trying to earn the money to pay back the investment. (Note how the depreciation element

▶

has increased for A.) At the same time, the competitor is virtually guaranteed to enjoy a competitive advantage – at company A's expense!

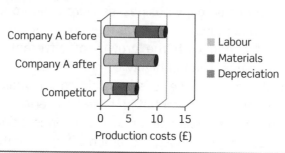

Try this

- Segment the market in terms of what customers value when they buy your products or services. Do this even when you are working on an initiative that is not directly market-facing.
- Translate this into competitive advantage ratings for the players in this market.
- Determine to what extent existing competitive advantages can be sustained.
- Identify implications of this for solution focus areas *and* minimum requirements for potential solutions.
- Generate alternative solutions within this framework.

Tip

Imagine you are joining the market as a new entrant. You can start from a clean slate. Using available market and industry knowledge, describe how a new entrant could disrupt the market and become a leading player over a period of time.

This exercise will lead to a clearer understanding of the 'rules of engagement' in your market. It may unveil some uncomfortable truths, but that's the whole point; it is better that you do this yourself than have a competitor do it for you! As an incumbent, apply these insights to generate unique ideas to bolster your competitive position.

Reflection

- How did it work?

- What will I do next time?

References

Porter ME (1985) *Competitive Advantage: Creating and Sustaining Superior Performance.* Free Press.
See http://www.carrotmuseum.co.uk/babycarrot.html#full

2.3 Think outside the box!

Why

Once you have determined that unique ideas are needed to set yourself apart from the competition, the question is how to get those unique ideas. The classic answer to this is to 'think outside the box'. This is often perceived as the preserve of a rare breed of blue-sky thinkers. Others regard it just as a red herring. Both notions are incorrect. To start with the latter, there is real practical value in this approach that can be applied to everyday situations. Just like when you are stuck and someone new to the situation joins in, a fresh pair of eyes can make a difference in unlocking the situation. Without being tied down by history, habit and assumptions (note: these are all box creators), their perspective can make you think of things you have simply overlooked before. This already makes the point that it is a lot easier to step out of your box with the help of someone else.

The exclusivity of outside-the-box thinking is also often overestimated. *Everyone* can think outside the box. The key point is this: once you have identified what your mental box is, you can step out of it and look at the situation from a wider perspective. It is all about acknowledging and letting go of perceived constraining factors to enable you to get new insights.

Business briefing

The term 'think outside the box' is thought to originate from the management consulting industry in the 1970s and 1980s when consultants used a nine-dot puzzle to encourage clients to think in lateral ways.

The puzzle proposed an intellectual challenge (see illustration below). This is easily resolved, but only by drawing the lines outside the confines of the square area defined by the nine dots themselves. The phrase 'thinking outside the box' is a restatement of the solution strategy. The puzzle only seems difficult because people commonly imagine a boundary ('the box') around the edge of the dot array. The heart of the matter is the unspecified barrier that people typically perceive.

The 'nine dots' puzzle. The goal of the puzzle is to link all nine dots using four straight lines, or fewer, without lifting the pen and without tracing the same line more than once.

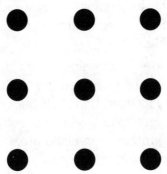

In business situations, this applies just as well. Specifying any perceived (and implicit) barriers crystallises what lies beyond them and questions whether they are valid. Very often the simple act of barrier-awareness opens people's minds to how to get over those barriers.

Try this

- Hold a short working session with the problem stakeholders. A half hour is sufficient in most cases.
- Ask each participant upfront to individually list what they see as the constraints and conditions to addressing the problem.
- The group absorbs all stakeholder inputs with a brief explanation. Questions can be asked for clarification, no critiquing or counter arguments permitted at this stage.
- Conclude the session with an overview of agreed constraints and the conditions under which they are valid.
- Use this as input for structured brainstorming sessions (see Section 2.5).

Tips

- Identifying your mental box is a lot easier when you work with others. Get them involved wherever you can, however briefly they are available.

- For problems you are addressing on your own, work in a space where you cannot be disturbed. Try to think aloud and say whatever is on your mind. Don't hold back hunches, guesses, wild ideas, images, plans or goals. Jot down key words and keep going rather than elaborate. Review your inputs afterwards to crystallise your box.

- Although a great concept, don't get complacent once you have identified your box and have stepped out of it. There is always another box! If you change the challenge from the nine-dot example to link all dots with just three lines, the boundaries of the paper become the box. With one line as the challenge, the size of the pen tip in relation to the nine dots becomes the box. Are you restless yet?

Reflection

- How did it work?

- What will I do next time?

Reference

Fleck JI and Weisberg RW (2004) The use of verbal protocols as data: An analysis of insight in the candle problem. *Memory & Cognition*, 32(6): 990–1006.

2.4 Focus on bigger problems to find bigger solutions

Why

Remember, we're still on a quest for unique ideas that will help us create, sustain or increase our competitive position. Where thinking outside the box typically helps us to think of the solutions a bit further afield, it also pays to ask whether we may be constrained in our solution creation by the way the problem has been framed. Note that we are not questioning anymore whether we are working on the right problem. That was the preserve of Chapter 1. Here we're simply asking ourselves what the solutions would look like if the problem was of a bigger magnitude.

Business briefing

In this section we are pulling a number of concepts together that we have used so far. How we identify the context for our problem really draws the first mental box for us. The larger and wider we set our context – assuming it stays relevant and manageable – the more room we give ourselves to consider bigger problems and the potential solutions to address them. We may not always want to address the biggest problem to the fullest extent, and that is not the point. The value of using this approach is to identify solutions that would otherwise not be considered. As a secondary benefit, it helps to put into context to what extent the problem you started working on at the outset merits being addressed compared to other priorities you identified as you went along.

Example

In *Jack: Straight from the Gut* former General Electric Chairman Jack Welch talks about many GE businesses celebrating their success at being the number one or two in their market. A golden rule for Mr Welch had been that GE businesses should either occupy a number one or two spot in a market or exit the GE group. This all changed once an outsider commented that this focus had led many GE businesses to define their markets such that they would demonstrably occupy a leading position in that market [note: mental box].

In other words, these businesses were being leaders in a self-created illusion. From this moment onwards, the challenge to GE businesses became to define their markets in such a way that their market share would only amount to 10 per cent – and then to create business plans to become a defining leader in those markets. This completely changed their mindsets and drove them to grow in multiples as opposed to percentages!

Try this

- Whatever your problem is, multiply it by a factor 10. Now brainstorm for possible solutions. Does this generate new ideas? Will those strategies also work for the current, smaller problem? What would deploying them allow you to achieve?
- Outline what you could do if you had twice the money to spend. What would be different? What would be the value of that be?

(People often balk at this question as being unrealistic – most companies want to get the job done for the lowest possible cost. My retort to that is that if it generates ideas with better returns on the investment you are making, you would *want* to make them happen. This presupposes of course that the organisation has the financial resources and manpower available to make that project a success.)

- The holistic perspective: address how this could be this part of a bigger question. If financially feasible solutions are hard to come by, this *may* point to the long-term feasibility of the underlying business activity being questionable. Is this perhaps the time to consider the start of a controlled wind-down?
- Alternatively, it may be a question of required scale. Is there a way you can virtually get to a bigger scale to justify the investment?

Example

In September 2014, four major industrial companies based near the Dutch city of Tilburg announced a joint investment in a shared sustainable wastewater purification installation. Water treatment will process approximately 10 million gallons per day. This joint wastewater treatment brings several advantages. The new installation has a low energy consumption. After purification, the waste water will be discharged into a local canal. In the future, more consideration will be given to further re-use the water with the businesses or other sustainable efforts within the region.

By using innovative techniques, the joint operating company will also review whether sludge released by the co-purification can be processed into biogas. The self-purification of waste water by the four companies frees up capacity at the communal sewage plant. Expanding communal water purification for the Tilburg region can therefore be delayed. In addition, the cost of wastewater treatment for the four companies will be reduced. The various company-specific substances in the wastewater (from food and drinks production, film and fragrances) provide opportunity for more effective and efficient means of purification. The local water board was involved in the initiative. Although it means less water processing revenues for the water board, the social benefits are enormous. Besides sustainability aspects, the improved water quality and quantity of the local water bodies are an important factor.

Tip

Countering the tenor of this section, sometimes it pays to ask whether the problem can be broken down into smaller pieces. This helps you identify the zone where addressing the current problem makes a real difference. If you're pretty close to that point, does that give you any clues about potential alternative solutions?

Example

A manufacturer was looking to spend $50m on a truck replacement programme. These trucks were used to ship products from plants to distribution centres and then on to customers. The decision to propose replacement was driven by the average age of the fleet. When looking into the 10 per cent of trucks that would be the most urgent *and* those that would contribute the most profit, it emerged that spending just $5m on essential replacements would suffice to address the needs of the business. This was enabled by reassigning existing trucks based on their remaining useful life and capabilities. Another contributor was the elimination of truck replacements that would otherwise be assigned to non-value added activities. Wow, quite a saving!

Source: Dudarev Mikhail/Shutterstock

Reflection

- How did it work?

- What will I do next time?

Reference

Welch J with Byrne J A (2001) *Jack: Straight from the Gut.* Warner Books.
For details on the waste water example, see: https://www.google.co
.uk/url?sa=t&rct=j&q=&esrc=s&source=web&cd=3&ved=0ahUKEwikr
5WKjI7LAhVJtRQKHRxyDcEQFggsMAI&url=http%3A%2F%2Fwww
.cocacolanederland.nl%2FbuildPDF.aspx%3FPDFID%3D373&
usg=AFQjCNFvOvervlSyH3fksRC6m1RLQylgyA&sig2=H30dge
DRGCBaeNRKkYUmMQ&cad=rja

2.5 Use clear ground rules for productive brainstorming

Why

Great ideas are not born in silos. Cross-functional brainstorming can be very quick, efficient and powerful. Participants need to understand how to get the most out of a brainstorm session. Following a few rules can make a profound difference generating productive output from brainstorm sessions.

Business briefing

In their book *Brainsteering,* Kevin and Shawn Coyne demystify the secrets and fallacies of brainstorming. All too often, a random group of people gets locked in a room, are told to think outside the box and reminded that there are no bad ideas.

Source: Pressmaster/Shutterstock

This approach is highly likely to become a dispiriting exercise in spawning near-random ideas with limited pay-off. By applying a few simple focus areas, brainstorming can be made significantly more productive.

Try this

- **Understand the real criteria** the company will use to make decisions about the resulting ideas. Are there any absolute restrictions or limitations?

- **Ask the right questions.** They should force your participants to take a new and unfamiliar perspective to help shake up their thinking. The questions should also clearly define the conceptual space your team will explore. In other words, make people aware of the mental boxes within which to look for solutions.

- **Pick people who can answer the questions** you're asking. As obvious as this may sound, participants are often invited because of their place in the organisation rather than for their specific (first-hand) knowledge.

Source: PanicAttack/Shutterstock

- **Divide and conquer.** Work with short sessions and small groups (3–5 people) to promote active contributions. Have them focus on one single question for up to a half hour.

Quarantine idea crushers like bosses, 'big mouths' and subject matter experts in separate groups.

- **Prepare your participants** for the likelihood that their subgroup may generate only two or three worthy ideas per question. Knowing those odds upfront will prevent participants from becoming discouraged.

- **Wrap up with shortlists.** Have each subgroup filter top ideas from its own work and have them share these with the full group for final inputs. Be clear to the group about how the winning ideas will be chosen and how they will learn about the final results.

- **Enable swift follow-up** by briefing senior executives on selection criteria upfront. A particularly motivating factor is to ensure any decisions, including rejections, are clearly explained to the participants.

Source: abimages/Shutterstock

Tip

Treat a brainstorming workshop as your one-shot chance to get it right. Be absolutely thorough on your preparation of a workshop. With the right guidance and stage-setting, this can quickly generate new insights and deliverable ideas. Get it wrong and you have missed not just this opportunity, but also demotivated participants about contributing to any future occasions. So, no pressure then!

Reflection

- How did it work?

```
┌─────────────────────────────────────────────┐
│                                             │
│                                             │
│                                             │
│                                             │
│                                             │
└─────────────────────────────────────────────┘
```

- What will I do next time?

```
┌─────────────────────────────────────────────┐
│                                             │
│                                             │
│                                             │
│                                             │
│                                             │
└─────────────────────────────────────────────┘
```

References

Coyne KP and Coyne ST (2011a) *Brainsteering: A Better Approach to Breakthrough Ideas.* HarperCollins.
Coyne KP and Coyne ST (2011b) Seven steps to better brainstorming. *McKinsey Quarterly*, March 2011 (adapted).

2.6 Give your alternatives an honest, fair chance

'Always be constructively discontent.'
(Muhtar Kent, Chairman and CEO, The Coca-Cola Company)

Why

If you have come this far, you have already gone through a lot of trouble getting some unique ideas on the table to address a situation. In the quest for delivering solutions that boost your competitive position, your biggest enemy right now is bias. Bias will affect anyone involved in screening these ideas for a recommendation. We can typically recognise some bias in others, but often fail in spotting our own. Setting clear evaluation criteria and angles upfront for screening ideas goes a long way in filtering out the most obvious forms of bias.

Business briefing

The brain can be a deceptive guide for rational decision making. In his book *Thinking, Fast and Slow*, Daniel Kahneman explains how our brain is programmed to preserve energy by taking shortcuts whenever it thinks it can get away with doing so. Decision making and the consciously thinking through of alternatives are activities with high blood sugar consumption. It is no wonder then that our brain will try to lighten the load wherever possible. This has led to a myriad of shortcuts.

There are countless articles and books that cover the cognitive biases that prevent us from giving our alternatives an honest, fair chance. I personally like the work Dan Lovallo and Olivier Sibony of McKinsey have done in categorising these biases in five practical and recognisable groups.

(1) Action-oriented biases – drive action less thoughtfully

- Excessive optimism about outcomes
- Overconfidence in our ability to affect future outcomes
- Neglect competitive responses in plans

Source: 123rf.com

(2) Interest biases – from conflicting incentives and affiliations

- Misaligned individual incentives foster support for subsidiary views at the expense of the overall interest of the company.
- Inappropriate attachments of individuals to people or (legacy) elements of the business, creating a misalignment of interests.
- Misaligned perception of corporate goals and their relative weight in trade-offs between them.

(3) Pattern-recognition biases – even when there aren't any links

- Confirmation bias: overweighting evidence consistent with a favoured belief.
- Management by example: generalising based on examples that are particularly recent or memorable.
- False analogies: relying on comparisons with situations that are not directly comparable.
- Storytelling: the tendency to remember and to believe more easily a set of facts when they are presented as part of a coherent story.

- Champion bias: the tendency to evaluate a plan or proposal based on the track record of the person presenting it, more than on the facts supporting it.[6]

Source: Sergey Nivens/Shutterstock

(4) Stability biases - favouring inertia in the face of uncertainty

- Anchoring and insufficient adjustment. Rooting oneself to an initial value, leading to insufficient adjustments of subsequent estimates.

- Loss aversion. The tendency to feel losses more acutely than gains of the same amount, making us more risk averse than a rational calculation would suggest.

- Sunk-cost fallacy. Paying attention to historical costs that are not recoverable when considering future courses of action.

- Status quo bias. Preference for the status quo in the absence of pressure to change it.

---

[6] A great illustration of this is the case described in *Decisive* of Quaker CEO William Smithburg getting his board to approve the disastrous acquisition of Snapple (bought for $1.8bn in 1994, sold for $300m three years later), largely on the basis of his very successful take-over of Gatorade a decade earlier. The fact that Snapple was a company with very different dynamics was ignored in the business case.

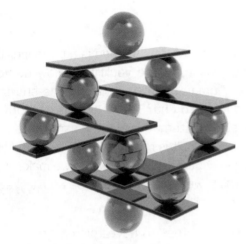

Source: ARTSILENSE/Shutterstock

(5) Social biases – arising from the preference for harmony over conflict

- Groupthink. Striving for consensus at the cost of a realistic appraisal of alternative courses of action.
- Sunflower management. Tendency for groups to align with the views of their leaders, whether expressed or assumed.

Source: Vasyl Dudenko/Shutterstock

Try this

Sit tight for a moment, this section is a bit longer than usual, but for good reason, I hope you'll find. How do you prevent the powerful human brain from taking the shortcuts it has programmed itself to find? The answer is deceptively simple: formally assess all alternatives by the same criteria, using the same rigour for each. It is relatively easy to verify whether the latter has been done. However, how can we make sure that the criteria by which we judge alternatives aren't skewed by our biases to favour certain solutions?

I'm not going to profess to have this challenge nailed down to perfection. That said, the following approaches make a noticeable difference in keeping you on the straight and narrow:

- Before embarking on a quest for solutions to your problem, identify (the) criteria that a solution needs to be screened against to suitably address the identified problem. Distinguish here between two different types of criteria.

- Firstly, create clarity about the 'must-pass' criteria. This can either be a binary in/out check or a minimum/maximum score on a metric. This lets you assess whether any alternative qualifies as a potential solution.

Source: Raywoo/Shutterstock

- Secondly, identify criteria that may help you to compare qualifying alternatives. These can either be nice-to-have aspects or relevant metrics where scores may vary. For anything measurable, be clear about the acceptable range within which potential solutions should score. For some metrics that may mean anything over a threshold or anything below a ceiling is acceptable. Whatever it is, think it through and spell it out.

If you use the Brainsteering approach discussed in Section 2.5, you will have done this already.

There is a good reason for setting criteria prior to looking for potential solutions. This way, you are reducing the chances of bias, allowing a particular solution to be favoured by your choice of screening criteria. Now, that's nice in theory, but chances are that you started this whole journey due to a potential solution rearing its head somewhere! That means that bias is already at work in some shape or form. To correct for this, and even if you didn't have a solution as your starting point, use an iterative approach. Once you have identified a long list of potential solutions, review them for their problem-solving capacity as well as potential side benefits and unintended consequences. This may lead you to include additional criteria that you would otherwise have overlooked.

Source: 123rf.com

The critical reader in you may remark that this opens the door to including criteria to give certain alternatives an unfair advantage in the comparison. And that's absolutely spot on. So let's be clear here. What we want is the best solution for the business. If an alternative achieves a lot more desirable benefits than we are asking for, this ought to be included in the assessment. Similarly, if a potential solution passes all the must-have criteria, but has any unintended and undesirable consequences elsewhere in the organisation, this needs to be acknowledged as well. The ultimate choice is still a trade-off between what the business needs most, what it can afford and what it is able to deliver. The better informed you are, the better you are equipped to make that choice.

This may result in you proposing a solution that is higher in cost, but better for the business overall. At other times you may find that for a fraction of the anticipated costs you can achieve the bulk of the required benefits and that the balance does not justify the marginal benefits it brings. The truck replacement example from Section 2.4 is a good illustration of the latter.

- Task someone, or, for larger projects, a team, with proving why a project should *not* go ahead, akin to a 'devil's advocate' role. This can focus either on disproving the urgency or importance of the problem, or on the merits of the proposed solution. With an awareness of the major biases as a starting point, this can bring balance to the decision-making process and reduce the influence of bias.[7]

- Whenever possible, assess your most compelling alternatives with a financial analysis of costs and benefits. The caveat here is that the analysis may overlook part of the solution's implications. This may be due to a too narrow focus. Alternatively, people may not feel comfortable or able to quantify 'softer' costs and benefits. I have personally witnessed numerous occasions where people took the stance that a solution was a strategic imperative that the business simply had to do, despite poor financial returns. But that is no reason not to give cost and

---

[7] See also Section 5.4.

benefit quantification a serious try.[8] After all, if a strategy is not making any money, it won't be sustainable for long.

Tips

- Be cautious of the pros vs cons comparison.[9] Its simplicity makes it a much used technique. Although it is quick to put together and easy to digest, it provides a false sense of giving honest, fair chances to alternatives. The approach is very prone to bias due to a number of factors:

  - it tends to be completed on a discretionary and inconsistent basis;
  - a check on the completeness of the final comparison is often missing;
  - users implicitly assume that every pro or con has the same weight;
  - occasionally, pros for one alternative can be interpreted as cons for other alternatives.

Source: woaiss/Shutterstock

---

[8] The techniques available for doing so go beyond the scope of this book. Interested readers should look into expected value calculation approaches, Point of View analyses and working with a Range of Outcomes.

[9] Documented as long ago as 1772 by Benjamin Franklin as 'Moral Algebra'.

- Steer clear of assigning weights to screening criteria unless you can prove the validity of the weighting proportions. Although weighting can be really helpful to ensure key factors get appropriate consideration, most weighting tends to be determined by a body of experts or company management. These groups are typically likely to be influenced by groupthink (bias).

  In addition, weighting tends to be used as a proxy for quantifying 'soft' benefits or strategic aspects, easily leading to erroneous conclusions on the desirability of given solutions (see last paragraph under 'Try this' above).

Reflection

- How did it work?

- What will I do next time?

References

Kahneman D (2011) *Thinking, Fast and Slow.* Farrar, Straus and Giroux.

Lovallo D and Sibony O (2010) A language to discuss biases. *McKinsey Quarterly*, March 2010.

Roxburgh C (2003) Hidden flaws in strategy. *McKinsey Quarterly*, 2: 27–40.

Sellers P (2012) Muhtar Kent's new Coke. *Fortune*, 10 May 2012.

2.7 Go on, do cherry pick

Why

All too often potential solutions are unwittingly regarded as mutually exclusive, especially when they are very similar to one another. Yet most times there is very little that would stop you from acting like a child in a sweet store and pick all the things you fancy. With a child's mindset, you can either end up choosing a number of actions to move forward at the same time, or, even, to ask for the best bits from each potential solution to be combined. Both approaches underscore the importance of consciously starting with a wide range of creative alternatives, so that you have something to choose from.

Source: gemphoto/Shutterstock

Business briefing

In Section 2.1 we identified that considering multiple alternatives adds significant value as it increases the odds for success by a factor of 6 compared to 'whether or not' decisions. Interestingly, the number of alternatives does not need to be large. Just two serious ones (lip-service doesn't count!) pitched against each other already drastically increases the odds for decision success. When we know that the average strategic project underdelivers by somewhere in the region of 40–50 per cent, that is no mean feat.

You may wonder why just looking at one additional alternative makes such a difference. This is materially explained by the cherry-picking from alternatives as described above.

When you give serious thought to multiple alternatives, you may find you want it all, or that you want to make the most of what's on offer. That mindset leads you to explore how you can make that happen. And if you don't quite like what you see, it's easier to ask for other solutions.

Contrast that to a 'whether or not' decision, where it's much easier to be lured into thinking that you need to argue a case either in favour or against the one proposal on the table, and persuaded to think that no changes are allowed. Yet it's often the changes and tweaks to initial ideas that make the chosen solution successful by integrating more insights.

Source: Dirk Ercken/Shutterstock

Try this

- Even though just two alternatives already make a difference, you'll initially need to look at a larger number that you can whittle down to a serious short list.

- When generating alternatives, make a specific effort to look at 'low-cost' and 'no-cost' solutions. These tend to be very suitable for parallel implementation, and may spark some ideas that can be bolted on to more resource-intensive solutions.

- Always ask the question why the Optimised Base Case shouldn't be implemented (first). See Section 3.6 to understand why.

- When screening alternatives, make a point of crystallising to what extent they can be combined with the other alternatives you are considering. Alternatively, ask how you can incorporate particularly desirable benefits of one alternative into another potential solution.

- For bigger initiatives, consider starting off with 'multi-tracking', where multiple teams separately generate sets of potential solutions before bringing them together to review them for 'AND' potential.

Example

Below is an example of a project where the team considered alternative solutions for a problem. In this situation, a production plant was running out of capacity. Look how many of the team's alternatives can be implemented fairly easily and at relatively low cost. Readers familiar with production line intricacies will know that the potential of the 'line tweak' alternatives is in part dependent on how well the line is run already. Yet, thinking these through in a concerted approach will quickly show where the biggest potential lies, and whether this is worth the effort.

▶

Alternatives
Invest in new production line
Increase production line efficiency
Line upgrading
Straight runs to minimise change-overs
Run more shifts
Toll-packing (by contractor)
Import (from sister company)
Delist stock keeping units to free up time on the line
Increase selling price

Note also how most of these could be implemented simultaneously in many similar situations. This underscores the notion of AND-AND vs OR-OR thinking and can really help to beat the odds of project success and delivering stronger results. In this situation, the 'big-ticket' alternative ultimately ended up being required. However, the thinking through of alternatives bought the business some time before having to embark on this. In addition, it helped the team think ahead about how to extract more value from an investment in a new line once the new line would be in operation.

Tips

- Even if an idea only addresses a part[10] of a problem, don't discard it just on those grounds. Sometimes when the biggest headache has been addressed, the rest of the problem becomes less of a priority and more or less goes away.

---

[10] In this context, 'part' should be read both as 'aspect' (qualitative) and 'partial' (quantitative).

- 'Partial' ideas may buy you time to address the problem with a bigger or better solution. In many situations buying time has value to either better understand how a problem should be solved, or to simply put the long-term solution in place.
- Combining a number of 'partial' ideas (the AND-AND approach) can give you a serious alternative to fully solving your problem.

Reflection

- How did it work?

- What will I do next time?

Chapter 3

What would you really, really do without money?

3.1 Make the most of what you have with the Optimised Base Case

We often aim for solutions that completely solve the problem or seize the opportunity. Most of the time, we already have tools at our disposal with which we can make significant inroads in achieving our goal. We can either use slack resources, or choose to do less of something we currently do and use the time to capture the opportunity at stake instead. Overlooking these tools is one of the big factors explaining why the average business project falls short of expectations.

Dutch artist Rob van Haandel (www.moox.nl) uses this approach by integrating wine glasses in his design for a lamp instead of their originally intended purpose.

Source: Rob van Haandel

Do this

Answer this question: 'What is the one thing we could do differently to enable us to seize all or part of the opportunity and not use any incremental funding or resources?'

3.2 Create real value, fast

Because working with an Optimised Base Case (OBC) typically means using your existing resources more or differently, it can unlock substantial value quicker than most 'clean slate' solutions. The hard work is in letting go of pre-conceived notions and making sometimes tough choices.

Source: ktsdesign/Shutterstock

Do this

Identify the elements of the OBC that you can do pretty much right away. How far will this get you?

3.3 Create instant credibility (1)

There's something powerful about the Optimised Base Case. It's your honest answer to how you would seize the opportunity at stake without using incremental resources. This gets you eye-to-eye with the truth. Stakeholders will recognise this as they get a better understanding of the trade-offs the organisation will have to make under this scenario. In your quest for the right decision, your Optimised Base Case is the cornerstone.

Source: Tonis Pan/Shutterstock

Do this
Identify the constraints you would come up against if you were to seize the opportunity with the OBC. What would it take for each constraint to evaporate?

3.4 Create instant credibility (2)

Many organisations unwittingly set themselves up for project disappointments by using the status quo as the baseline against which they measure the incremental costs and benefits of potential solutions. This approach completely ignores the value that is within ready reach through deploying the Optimised Base Case. Measure the value of any project against the Optimised Base Case instead, and you will automatically avoid double-counting some of your gains. A great start to any project, and a strong credibility booster.

What would you really, really do without money?

Source: Anna Hoychuk/Shutterstock

Do this

Describe your OBC as clearly as possible. Focus on what will be different from today's situation, what trade-offs you are making and how this achieves the targeted benefits within the constraints of the OBC.

3.5 Unveil value in projects you'd normally avoid

It may be counter-intuitive, but the bulk of the financially most attractive projects is made up by – on the face of it – unexciting opportunities. Projects that replace ageing assets or avoid potential future cost increases are often ignored until it is too late. Leverage insights from the OBC to spot the right 'ugly ducklings' before you kill the goose that lays the golden egg.

Source: Photodisc

Do this
Keep a cool head when dealing with 'hot potatoes'. Most projects being avoided need doing at some point anyway. Develop a point of view on the timing or circumstances for taking action on these.

3.6 Be clear on why *not* to do the Optimised Base Case

By its very nature, the Optimised Base Case is typically one of the cheapest solutions and also one bearing a lower risk profile. Especially in situations of high uncertainty, the benefit of buying time with a low-cost initial solution will often stand out. Yet, there are also situations where going slow is not the right answer, where the benefits are not that material or where implementing the OBC is too disruptive on the current set of activities.

Source: Becky Stares/Shutterstock

Do this

Use your senses. If the OBC makes you nervous, you're probably right. Articulate why and use this to justify your investment case.

3.7 Harvest insights gained from the Optimised Base Case

You may or may not end up embarking on the opportunity. And even if you do, you may or may not put the Optimised Base Case forward as the recommended solution. In any case, you are bound to gain or sharpen insights about your current business model or its environment when you develop the Optimised Base Case. Capture, crystallise and leverage these, whatever you end up doing.

Source: Kletr/Shutterstock

Do this

Play out the implications of your OBC on customers and suppliers. Are you leaving money on the table?

BIG PICTURE

3. What would you really, really do without money?

3.1 Make the most of what you have with the Optimised Base Case

Why

Very often, using our existing tools and resources in a different way is overlooked when it comes to addressing problems. If considered, people will typically come from the position that their business is already continually optimising resources anyway and that no further benefit can be gained.

But that stance misses the notion that a new lens is shaped by the problem at hand. And looking at the world through this lens may well unveil opportunities of creating value with existing tools and resources where that value exceeds the value generated by how those tools are being used at the moment.

Source: Jo Ann Snover/ Shutterstock

What would you really, really do without money?

There are plenty of situations where selecting the Optimised Base Case would not be preferred. Typical reasons relate to having limited scope for solving the problem, either value- or scale-driven. But whenever the Optimised Base Case is used as part of the chosen solution, the exciting bits are (1) crystallising value from – in hindsight – apparently obvious sources, and (2) the short time-to-value. After all, an OBC is only an OBC if you can do it pretty much right away.

Business briefing

The Optimised Base Case interestingly originated from operations management. When running a production line, the beauty of a thought-out weekly production schedule is often interrupted by the reality of daily life. Rush orders get placed and it is up to the operating team to optimise the situation, using the production schedule as their baseline. This is typically a constrained environment where production capacity is sparse. Every change in product produced is likely to incur downtime on the line to allow for changes in parts, moulds or materials. More downtime means less available production time.

'Making the most of what you have' is therefore the device. This is a balancing act between managing short-term customer satisfaction and long-term profitability. To be sustainably successful in optimising the base case, the team needs to have an unequivocal understanding of business priorities and value drivers. This often results in finding ways to do more with the same resources and in making conscious choices about what to do less of in favour of a more valuable activity.

Try this

- Answer this question: 'What would we really, really do if we didn't have access to incremental resources and still wanted to seize all or part of the opportunity to maximise profit?'
- Describe the answer thoroughly, focusing particularly on trade-offs that you may need to make.

- Explore potential second-order impacts your choices may lead to.[1]
- Be courageous enough to venture into extreme scenarios. Examples are:
  - What if we used our entire advertising budget for this year to hire extra sales people instead?
  - Let's stop making army tanks and use our production lines for producing tractors for agriculture in difficult terrain.
- Identify what proportion of each current business activity relevant for your problem is the most valuable. This is a Pareto analysis of sorts. Not every hour spent on each current activity has the same value. What is the point where value is maximised? Can you afford giving up the proportion that adds little value? Knowing this helps you understand potential inflection points and which trade-offs are worth making. The truck example in Section 2.4 is a great illustration of using this insight.[2]
- Consolidate your insights into a scenario that is your answer to the *really, really* question. Sometimes an OBC will get you far enough not to want to bother with alternative solutions for some time. In other cases the potential upheaval, likely a largely hidden cost, may dwarf the expected benefits of the OBC.

---

[1] An example of second-order impacts is the publication of executive remuneration in major corporations. In 2006, unions in the UK saw their long-standing efforts rewarded in getting companies to report senior executive pay in their annual filings. The Companies Act made it a legal requirement to do so for any listed company. The underlying thought was that if this was public information, companies would show more restraint in how senior executives are rewarded, as they were expected to align with the pay review of other workers. Interestingly, the availability of this information enabled many executives to negotiate better packages on the basis of comparison with alleged peers. Over the period 1998–2010, executive pay has increased 13.6% per year – markedly higher than the 4.7 per cent for average workers. Similar patterns have emerged in other countries. Not quite what the unions intended! (https://www.gov.uk/government/uploads/system/uploads/attachment_data/file/31360/12-889-improved-transparency-executive-remuneration-impact.pdf).

[2] This is a great example of the insights from the Optimised Base Case leading to a vast reduction of the business case for investment. Over time, on its own, the Optimised Base Case would lead to a reduction in available trucks from regular wear and tear, despite the positive impacts of the OBC. As a result, the business would suffer from *just* implementing the OBC. However, deploying the insights from the OBC enabled the manufacturer to reduce the investment amount in his fleet by about 90%.

What would you really, really do without money?

Reflection

- How did it work?

- What will I do next time?

3.2 Create real value, fast

'If you are not creating value for others then you are wasting your time.'

(Bryant H. McGill, American author)

Why

Your natural inhibitors to developing an OBC are driven by the extent to which you are willing to embrace the adagio 'Out with the old, in with the new'. Note, I'm not propagating this for the sake of favouring 'the new' by default. It's simply a requirement to give the OBC a serious chance. The reward for doing so lies in the OBC often being your fastest route to creating any value. The reason for this is simple. The most critical elements to making your OBC work are often already in place. All that is needed is choosing how to deploy them, possibly enabled by a few tweaks.

The magnitude of OBC benefits may vary from case by case, but, all other things being equal, there's no denying the desirability over more value virtually now compared to more value at some point further in the future.

Business briefing

The two critical requirements for the OBC are:

1. It's what you would really, really do in the absence of incremental resources, and

2. You can do it pretty much right away, bar perhaps a few enabling tweaks to your existing situation. Distilling the insight and making trade-offs is the hard part.

Really, really

When you think about it for a moment, both make a lot of sense. If you are looking at something that is not readily accepted by the key stakeholders as something you would realistically do, then the benefits of that scenario are not the ones to use as the baseline to compare investment cases against. After all, if the baseline is questionable, this leaves room for interpretation of the benefits that are derived by the initiative.

In that case you should expect benefits to evaporate as the project progresses. Implementers simply don't feel accountable to a hypothetical baseline. It is much better to have an OBC that everyone accepts as the best you could get already, and that only any benefits achieved over and beyond the OBC should be attributed to alternative solutions.

Right away

The ability to do something right away is important, as it underscores the notion of within-reach benefits. In assessing the OBC opportunity, reality comes into play here. Doing something right away is not an objective in its own right. It needs to be considered in the context of what is realistically possible. If, for example, you would technically be able to stop making a certain product right away (to free up production capacity for a different product), but contractual obligations require you to give a large customer nine months' notice to terminate, you might wonder whether this scenario is still OBC material. The answer is, it depends.

First of all, proportionality plays a role, both in terms of time and of magnitude. If any alternative solutions will take materially longer to implement, then the nine-month lead time could still be a decent OBC scenario. The proviso is that such lead time is pure lead time to get the scenario up and running.

Also, if some relatively small payments need to be made for, say, change parts, you could regard this as an OBC scenario, particularly when those investments are proportionately small compared to a fully-fledged project investment.

Secondly, relevance comes into play. Just like with any other alternatives, the OBC is not something that gets drafted up once to then be used 'as is'. That would risk it becoming an academic exercise. The purpose is to find real value here. You want to look, pick and choose the combination that actually works for an OBC. So if you would be able to start the OBC with smaller volumes right away, and then ramp up once the earlier-mentioned customer commitment has been fulfilled, that would be an example of a phased OBC taking real-life constraints into account.

Try this

- Treat the development of the OBC as your *one shot* to seize the opportunity. This dedicated focus is needed to crystallise sources of value from your existing set of circumstances.

- For bigger projects, or where the project team has difficulty to seriously engage with the OBC, appoint a separate team to develop the OBC.

- Be clear that, if this was your business, the proposed OBC is what you would really, really do to seize the opportunity with existing means. For a convincing case, develop a well-founded point of view on which resources can be used and why. This is particularly important if those resources are currently clearly adding value to the business already. Has the cost and impact of resource reallocation been thought through?

- Translate this into a value delivery plan: how will you make sure that the benefits ultimately translate into cash?[3]

- Look consciously for opportunities to combine parts of the OBC with alternative solutions. This typically contributes to the early realisation of benefits from incremental solutions.

Tips

- Know when to stop. With all the implied praise for the OBC, you'd be forgiven for thinking it is the one-stop answer to every problem. When there are either no accessible suitable resources in the current set-up, or when the OBC's use of those resources generates less value than you currently do, there's clearly no point in progressing with the OBC.

- If the notion of no incremental resources being available feels too unrealistic for you, work with the following assumption: for

▶

---

[3] For projects where cash delivery is not immediately relevant, focus on a benefit delivery plan.

the next three years all incremental resources will be dedicated to a highly strategic multi-year project. Any initiatives outside that project must be managed from within the business' current set of resources for this period. Can you afford to wait on the opportunity for three years? Or is there a way that you can make in-roads into the opportunity so that you are ready for a more strategic step when resources are available again? The OBC analysis will help you prove what makes sense to do for the intermittent period.

Reflection

- How did it work?

- What will I do next time?

3.3 Create instant credibility (1)

'Everyone wishes to have truth on his side, but not everyone wishes to be on the side of truth.'

(Richard Whately, Archbishop of Dublin (1787–1863))

Why

The majority of business projects end up disappointing on one or more of the fronts of cost overruns, results delivery or timely completion. Decision makers are therefore rightly questioning why your project should be any different. You need to establish credibility in order for decision makers to be willing to at least entertain the idea of going along with you. When you develop the OBC, you tackle this question with two distinct prongs.

Business briefing

Firstly, when you develop your OBC, you end up exposing a number of business fundamentals. After all, you are exploring the boundaries of possibility within your existing set of circumstances. These fundamentals can relate to the nature of your business, industry or market. Some may be well known, others a refreshing new insight. Whatever they are, people will recognise them as truths as soon as they see them. This recognition may be preceded by some reluctance in cases where previous decisions or current practice are called into question. Whether initially liked or not, the crystallisation of undeniable truths is a cornerstone for establishing the credibility of your business case.

> **Credibility** /krɛdɪˈbɪlɪti/ noun *the quality of being trusted and believed in.*

Secondly, taking the approach to first 'clean up the house' demonstrates an earnestness to only ask for incremental resources when there's a proven need for them. It displays ownership thinking and a willingness to do some hard work of the slow thinking[4] type, as opposed to 'throwing money at the problem' out of convenience. Although many people claim they will be thinking like an owner, stakeholders will recognise you putting your money where your mouth is through your efforts to develop a true OBC. And that is another string to your credibility bow.

---

[4] See Section 2.6.

Try this

- Take mental distance from the way things are being done today. Perhaps you were involved in creating the situation that exists today. Whether you were or weren't, let's assume that what is in place today was put there by acting with the best intentions on the best possible knowledge and insights available at the time. But that was then. With a new opportunity (or problem) looming on the horizon, we need to reconsider whether what we have right now could be put to better use to maximise its utility to the business.

- Identify the constraints you would come up against if you would try to seize the opportunity with the OBC. These can be constraints in your operations, your industry or your market.

- Clarify what it would take for that constraint to evaporate. Even if the answer is ridiculous at first sight, do record it.

- Rank every step in order of their cost/benefit ratio, from low to high.[5] Describe your OBC in that order, distinguishing between definite inclusions, potential inclusions and definite exclusions.

- Reality-test your assessment, don't just work with a paper cost/benefit analysis. Obtain alignment from those that would need to make the OBC work. How far are they willing to go down your list of actions, and why? Are they prepared to support the implementation of the OBC if the business elected to take that route?

---

[5] For incremental solutions, you would include feasibility in an analysis such as this to prioritise your actions. For the OBC, one of the critical requirements is that you should be able to do it pretty much right away. That takes feasibility out of the equation for the OBC. This is different from probability of success – for an illustration, refer to the case study about boxes vs shrink film in Section 3.7.

Tips

- Stay factual. No matter how much you *know* you have truth on your side, there's no need to 'rub it in'. Sometimes the truths you uncover can initially make stakeholders quite uncomfortable. The easier you make it for others to acknowledge your insights without losing face, the easier it will be for them to support your business case.

- Where there is room for interpretation, be open and upfront about this. Identify whether this is a must-know item before proceeding, or can you live with an approximation or a confirmation at a later date?

- Invite inputs from others. The more they engage, the more they are likely to put effort in to improve the proposal. That engagement may even lead to fundamental changes to your proposal. Welcome this. After all, what we want is the best solution for the business. Even if that means the end result is very different from what you envisaged, that's OK.

Reflection

- How did it work?

What would you really, really do without money?

- What will I do next time?

┌───┐
│   │
│   │
│   │
│   │
│   │
└───┘

3.4 Create instant credibility (2)

'The truth always turns out to be simpler than you thought.'
(Richard P. Feynman, US theoretical physicist)

Why

The OBC is such a powerful tool not only because it is such a credible and feasible case. It also strongly contributes to the credibility of any incremental solution. It does so by eliminating the double-counting of benefits – the key reason for explaining underdelivery of project results.

Business briefing

The OBC puts a serious reality check on incremental initiatives. In many situations an incremental solution can deliver a benefit that can to an extent also be delivered by the OBC. Alternatives are rarely fully comparable on an apples-to-apples basis. Any benefit value additional to today's situation that the OBC can deliver is value that cannot be claimed as a benefit by an incremental solution. Only benefit value beyond the reach of the OBC can be rightfully attributed to incremental solutions.

By taking this approach, you prevent the business from double-counting benefits. This is one of the key reasons why the average project underdelivers; the benefit potential is partly already within reach. Although this makes incremental projects less attractive than they may initially have looked, it also makes them more credible. And credible project profiles allow for more reliable comparisons and, crucially, better prioritisation of projects.

Example

A manufacturer of ready meals has spotted a new trend and sees an opportunity to drive revenue growth through the introduction of luxury dine-at-home meals. In the OBC, part of the opportunity can be addressed by using spare capacity on an existing production line. Increased production change-overs would make this more costly from an operations perspective, as there would be more hours where the line's crew spends time cleaning and preparing the machine for another product instead of actually producing saleable product. The favoured incremental alternative is to invest in an additional production line tailored to the requirements of the luxury dine-at-home market. This will involve lower on-going operational costs (less production change-overs, modern equipment) and provides capacity to grow.

Operating income (profit) comparison of OBC and investment case (incremental income)

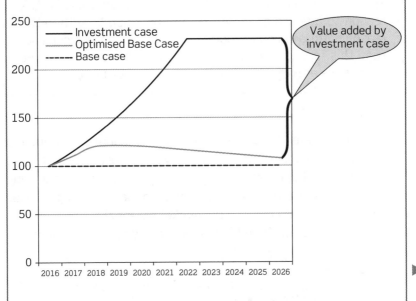

The chart above compares the total profit the company would be making under the base case ('Do Nothing'), the Optimised Base Case and the investment case.

The OBC here depicts a situation where the profit generated by the company goes up in the first two years as a result of volume growth. Once current capacity is utilised, profit is maximised. Over time, profit starts to decline as a result of ageing equipment requiring more maintenance stops. Maintenance is a double-edged sword; it costs money to perform *and* prevents you from generating saleable product during the stops. However, not doing maintenance is not an option either. As a result, annual profit declines over time.

The investment case curve depicts a slightly higher profit in the early years compared to the OBC on account of (a) less stops for production changes, and (b) working with more modern, efficient equipment. Profit growth stops once the machine has reached full capacity. Now, if you accept that the OBC's profit potential is already within reach, then that should become the baseline you compare the investment case against, rather than the base case. Making this new comparison, it becomes immediately apparent that in the first two years there is little reason to operate an incremental production line. The little reason there is becomes more questionable when we consider that this is a new market segment and that our volume projections are highly likely to be influenced by biases.[6]

In cases where there is any uncertainty about sales volume projections, anecdotal decision history suggests they are likely[7] to be overstated. In those cases, you would be better off launching the product using your existing production line first. Doing so gives you an opportunity to prove the market potential exists. With your knowledge gained from that launch, the decision to invest in a

---

[6] See Section 2.6.

[7] This is not always the case. Refer to Section 5.6 for using a Range of Outcomes in dealing with uncertainty.

new line can then be revisited at the right time with a markedly higher degree of credibility.

For readers with a financial background, this will make a lot of sense from the perspective of Net Present Value. The first years of a project carry the highest weight in the Net Present Value (NPV) calculation. If those first years contribute relatively little (in this example only 25–50 per cent of the incremental profit achieved in the year the existing capacity runs out), you would rather keep your money in the bank (or invested in quicker-return projects) than 'parking' it with an opportunity that you could also seize without investment.

As always, using tools consciously and with a constructively critical mind is important. In the above example, the conclusion to initially favour the OBC is relatively straightforward. However, for situations where the choice is not so clear-cut, try to focus in your decision analysis on the areas that contain the greatest relevant uncertainty.

In situations similar to the dine-at-home example, obvious candidates for extra analytical focus are parameters such as the time it takes to order new equipment, and volume forecast reliability. Refer to Chapter 6 for insights about productively dealing with risk and uncertainty.

Try this

- Start with the OBC that you have identified. Describe it as clearly and comprehensively as possible. Focus on what will be different from today's situation, what trade-offs you are making and how you expect to achieve the targeted benefits within the constraints of the OBC.

- For the investment case(s), describe the scope of the solution and its expected benefits. Where the OBC has the same type of benefit, be clear about the difference in the quantity of that benefit in both cases and the reason for this difference. You may find that the investment case includes benefit types that the OBC does not have. If so, validate whether these benefits could to an extent be achieved by widening the scope of the OBC.[8]

- Consolidate the credibility of the investment case by crystallising its incremental value over the OBC. This should go hand-in-hand with addressing the deliverability of that value. Give specific consideration to the timing and risk aspects of each case.

Tip

Start by describing your cases in words, pictures and diagrams. Paint a complete picture of both cases. No matter how tempting it is to start the comparison on a spread sheet, get a clear and complete understanding of the proposed case and its implications on the rest of the business first. This has two benefits: (a) it allows others to better understand (and challenge!) the intricacies and implications of each case; (b) you are in a better place to put together a credible, comprehensive financial analysis.

Reflection

- How did it work?

---

[8] This illustrates that crafting a business case is very much a dynamic activity. For as long as we can practically afford it, we continue to question whether our cases are the very best they can be.

- What will I do next time?

[ ]

3.5 Unveil value in projects you'd normally avoid

'All that is human must retrograde if it does not advance.'
(Edward Gibbon, English historian of Rome, 1737–1794)

Why

In many businesses you can find a pattern where replacement or defensive maintenance investments are put off as long as the business gets away with doing so. Often, the hidden problem with that is an ever-increasing cost structure, either in absolute or comparative terms. Colleagues are typically aware of the desirability to get things fixed. However, doing so will take resources away from more exciting initiatives. The OBC can lay bare the hidden cost of not taking action and helps find the right priority and timing for taking the proverbial bull by the horns.

Business briefing

Most people understand the concept 'first things first', epitomised as 'habit 3' in Stephen Covey's book *The 7 Habits of Highly Effective People.* The premise of 'first things first' is to prioritise the things that are urgent and important over everything else. In order to be able to do so, you need to be clear about what is important. Urgent things typically have a way of making themselves known, even though they may include some 'false positives' you may want to validate.

Look after what you have

For the majority of businesses, whatever brings in most of the money today has the potential to play that role in the foreseeable future. This 'cash-cow' is important to nurture. It ensures business continuity and affords the business to make in-roads into new markets, innovation or other types of expansion. On the market-facing side of business, a similar principle applies where sales people frequently report that it is much easier to sell to existing customers than it is to sell to new customers.

Despite the obvious rationale for 'looking after what you have', decisions to do so are often put off as long as possible. I regularly come across two explanations:

1. Tackling an issue to keep what you have is often less exciting than embarking on something new. Human nature simply causes us to keep these opportunities at bay.

2. The financial benefits of doing so are often regarded as unattractive.

Regarding the first point, the insights from Section 2.4 (Focus on bigger problems to find bigger solutions) will typically make this a little more exciting.

Ensure your perspective is valid

That these initiatives are regarded as financially unattractive is often caused by businesses taking a static view instead of looking dynamically at how costs and profit evolve. The following analogy makes that clear.

If you were tasked to buy a quantity of pants for a four-year old today that would last him a decade, you wouldn't get very far by buying pants of the child's current size for the next ten years (a typical analysis period for capital investment projects). Leaving rare exceptions aside, we know the child is going to grow and require larger-sized pants over time.

Swapping the child for a machine, we know that wear and tear will deteriorate a machine over time, causing it to require more costly maintenance stops and spare part replacements. In other words, even if we don't do anything, our cost structure is more likely to worsen over time than it is to stay as it is. On top of that, if the machine were to incur a critical failure, how would the business cope with that? This often involves outsourcing product (costly!) to sustain sales, lost sales (costly!), emergency repairs (costly!) and unplanned equipment replacement (costly!).

Example

The following graph shows how you would use an OBC in a cost avoidance scenario. Just like in a situation of incremental income, the base case here assumes that the company's profit will stay the same for the foreseeable future. The investment case reflects that you would be investing in a technologically more advanced piece of equipment compared to what you are replacing. As a result, the equipment will be more efficient. Perhaps it also runs a little faster or enables you to deliver quality benefits worth paying for. This is reflected in the P&L by a declining cost structure and an inversely related increase in profit as shown in the profit curve in the chart.

Operating income (profit) comparison of OBC and investment case (loss avoidance)

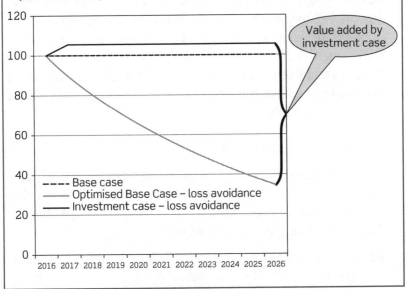

Blessed by ignorance of the OBC, most businesses would traditionally look at the difference between base case and investment case, and decide that, financially, making a replacement investment is not a priority. This view will be even stronger when the company also has investment opportunities chasing incremental revenue such as the example in Section 3.4. By contrast, the OBC reflects what is expected to happen to profit levels when current resources are used to maximise profit. In this example you see profit decline by about two thirds over the span of a decade as a result of 'making the most of what we've got', the OBC. Now, if you compare the investment case to the OBC, including the previously hidden value makes it immediately obvious that the replacement investment may actually be quite attractive.

Staying honest

For anyone wanting to 'help' the idea of a replacement investment gain acceptance, it can be very tempting to paint a dramatic picture here with rapid profit decline in the OBC. It is therefore worth planting a reminder that developing the OBC is done to help us take the best decision. It may well be that our best thinking about an OBC crystallises a picture that says: 'Actually, we will manage just fine for the next few years with some appropriate risk management and mitigation plans in place.' In that case, the OBC has helped you prove that, for the moment, it makes more sense to keep things as they are, perhaps resulting in a few tweaks from insights you picked up as a result of developing the OBC.

Putting it in perspective

You'll be forgiven for getting a little uneasy by now. Critical failures are rare, a bit of risk planning may well contain their cost and it's tricky to base an investment on something that *might* happen. That is absolutely true. My retort to that is:

(a) Low probabilities are no excuse for ignoring issues, especially when their impact can be devastating.

(b) Most businesses don't do sufficient contingency planning for critical failures. Most contingency plans are based on full sites being temporarily or permanently incapacitated. However, a critical failure of one production line or IT system has its own set of dimensions that is often overlooked in a business contingency plan.

(c) When it comes to probabilities, for most pieces of equipment and systems, a critical failure is merely a question of time. When you know that something undesirable is coming your way, you ought to have a point of view on what is the right time and approach to address it.

Try this

- The most important thing to do for an OBC on a cost avoidance opportunity is to agree with stakeholders on what the OBC looks like. Stakeholders are likely to have divergent views, influenced by interests, bias and experience. Getting this right is critical. No one wants to be in a position a few years down the road to say 'I told you so', when you ended up working with an OBC that turned out to be too optimistic about the remaining value from the asset at stake. At the same time, an overly pessimistic OBC risks being incredible – the very attribute the OBC should bring into the mix in the first place!

- Agree to disagree, should stakeholders not be able to get aligned on the OBC. Instead of working with an agreed OBC, work with a range from the most conservative to the most aggressive. Make sure that the full array of views gets captured in your analysis. Overlay on that range an assessment of what the difference between OBC and investment case needs to be to make the investment case a viable one (indicated by the horizontal line in the chart below). Do this preferably in financial terms, but other practical measures can also be considered.

▶

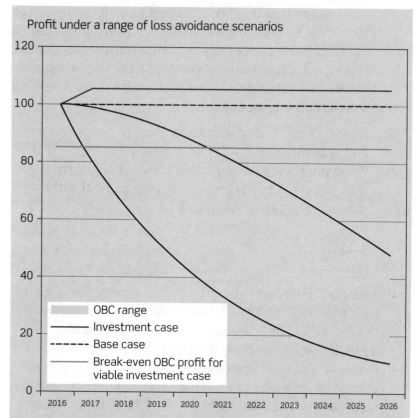

Profit under a range of loss avoidance scenarios

The outcomes of this analysis require some interpretation:

- 'No-brainer' situations. If the conservative end of the OBC range (upper curved line) already justifies making the investment, then the necessity of the investment should not be a point of contention. Conversely, if even the aggressive end of the OBC range (lower curved line) is not sufficient to make the investment case work, you're left with no choice but to live with what you have or to find a more affordable solution.

- Informed discussion. If the minimum required profit gap between OBC and investment case is somewhere within the OBC range, the discussion should focus on making this insight useful. It is likely that disagreement focuses on the timing of events of increasing failure. In that case, direct your energies to identify trigger points instead. The starting point then is that the OBC does not justify making an investment *now*. Identify what must happen for the business to want to make the investment, regardless of when we think this will happen. Then set a 'trip wire'[9] that leaves enough time to put the investment plan in place when the investment needs to be operational.

In the graph above, the horizontal line falls in this category. Note that the line depicts the *average* required profit for the investment case to break even.[10] A bigger profit gap between investment case and OBC would make a stronger case for investing. In the graph, it looks like the conservative end of the range could possibly meet this. In the early years it is above the break-even profit level, in the later years it falls well below. However it would take about 4–5 years to get to an 'in the money' situation. Is that an acceptable time? Or is there sufficient support among the stakeholders for the view that the avoided losses would be higher than the conservative case – and support making the investment sooner rather than later?

- Back to the drawing board. There will be situations where either the range is too wide or where there is strong disagreement over where in the range the outcomes are going to fall. To avoid hasty, wrong decisions or protracted unproductive discussions, focus your energy on finding smaller step-solutions. A large driver for loss avoidance situations is the need to contain and mitigate business risks. In stalemate situations, try to 'book-end' the risk by putting options and mitigation plans in place. Are there early warning signs or trigger points you can look out for to know when the time is right to reconsider the case? Last but not least, look

▶

---

9 See Section 6.6.

10 We use average annual profit here as a workable proxy to *visualise* the break-even profit level. Using a break-even curve with evolving profit figures would in most cases not match the level of accuracy this implies. Project case projections may fluctuate on either side of the curve. An OBC above the break-even level does not necessarily imply that the investment only makes sense once the lines cross. Remember we're dealing with uncertainty about the range here. To facilitate decision-making, translate cases into NPV figures for easy comparison.

What would you really, really do without money?

at your range of solutions. Are there smaller solutions you can put in place to alleviate the most pressing problems – and buy you some time to learn how the bigger problems may evolve? Or, are there much bigger solutions[11] (either in cost, scope or both) that would remove the business risk at the same time?

Tip

Look out for 'orphaned' problems. The impact of avoiding timely action is often exacerbated in the areas of infrastructure or overhead that support multiple profit streams. As no one feels responsible for maintaining something even as basic as a roof, a boiler house or a computer network, businesses often end up waiting until it threatens to destroy the very existence of the business.

Confusion alert

When users are first introduced to the OBC in incremental revenue situations, they understand quite quickly why the OBC is optimised compared to the base case – it depicts after all a situation that is an improved version of the base case.

However, confusion may reign in loss avoidance situations. It seems counter-intuitive that the Optimised Base Case displays a lower business profit profile than the base case. How is that optimised? Well, it's not. First of all, what many refer to as the base case is really what you should call the status quo, meaning everything stays exactly as it is well into the future. The base case on the other hand depicts the 'do nothing' scenario. And – with reference to the pant-buying analogy above – doing nothing most of the time does not mean that everything stays the same. It rather depicts a scenario of declining value over time.

The base case then is the *unseen* line in the graph above, of which the OBC depicts what you would really, really do to avoid as much

---

[11] See Section 2.4.

of the business risk for as long as possible without committing any incremental resources.

Reflection

- How did it work?

- What will I do next time?

Reference

Covey S (1989) *The 7 Habits of Highly Effective People: Powerful Lessons in Personal Change*. Free Press.

3.6 Be clear on why *not* to do the Optimised Base Case

Why

By now, you may have the impression that the OBC is a panacea for just about every problem. Well, no. The OBC is a tool that has its limitations besides its obvious benefits. Understanding the limitations is critical in you successfully using the OBC as part of your decision toolkit, time after time.

Business briefing

As a tool, I find the OBC overlooked in many businesses. At the same time, it often brings in immediate economic value when applied. Therefore, I put a lot of emphasis on it in my workshops, consultancy work and writing.

The primary use of the OBC is to develop a relevant point of comparison for any new project or investment ideas. The reason for doing so is that many projects disappoint in their delivery because part of that value could already be (and often ends up being) captured by existing resources. The OBC therefore aims to help you identify the true incremental value potential of new initiatives.

In their enthusiasm for the OBC, users may feel that they have to always recommend the OBC as part of the proposed solution. The truth is that not every situation lends itself for that. The OBC is particularly likely to be a good first solution when the OBC analysis has identified either:

(a) slack in the existing situation,

(b) a better use of currently deployed resources, or

(c) a markedly lower risk profile for the OBC compared to an incremental solution.

The potential identified by the OBC partly depends on the lens of opportunity through which it is developed.[12] If that lens does not offer a drastically different view to what the business is doing already, the opportunity to better use currently deployed resources is likely to be limited. You would then rather propose an incremental solution and capture more benefits that way.

Limited availability of slack resources is another factor in constraining the potential for OBC solutions. If a situation is efficiently set up and yields good value, then there is typically less

---

[12] See Section 3.1.

to optimise. Also OBCs that would be too disruptive on the current set of activities are unlikely candidates to be put forward. And that makes a lot of sense, because an OBC should be a low-or-no-cost solution that you can pretty much do right away. Anything that is disruptive to current valuable activities normally carries a (hidden) cost. That means such a scenario is:

(a) not quite do-pretty-much-right-away and

(b) not quite low-or-no-cost.

In those cases, you use the OBC primarily as a tool to establish credibility for your investment case. It proves after all that you are using your existing resources in a value-adding manner.

Try this

- Be sure to develop a proper OBC and steer clear of a short-cut assumption that the business is already doing all it can with its existing resources. To do this, identify the existing resources that you could use to seize the opportunity and crystallise the value that they currently add. Compare that to the value that they would add if they were deployed on seizing the opportunity instead.

- If there are any switching costs, capture them. These may be explicit costs or harder to quantify hidden costs.

- For any hidden switching costs, identify the value that you can afford them to be at. Compare that to your estimate of what they may be. Where needed, work with a range for an estimate.

- Compare risk and timing issues for each case you consider. These will typically have a monetary value, although they may take some skill to translate into a number. If you can find even an approximate value for them, you will make an informed decision on the fate of the OBC with a lot more confidence.

What would you really, really do without money?

Reflection

• How did it work?

• What will I do next time?

---

[13] Yes, typical, but not exclusive and not always.

3.7 Harvest insights gained from the Optimised Base Case

Why

Developing an OBC is like going on a treasure hunt. With a new lens and an inquisitive mind you should not be surprised at finding a treasure trove of insights that you can put to immediate use.

Business briefing

The thinking behind the OBC concept has strong connections with operations excellence (OE) and Six Sigma approaches. And that makes sense, because they all originate from the operations management discipline.

There is, however, a profound difference as well. OE and Six Sigma focus primarily on improving current systems, processes and procedures. You could loosely – and perhaps somewhat unkindly – summarise this as 'squeezing out slack'.

In addition, the OBC explicitly aims to identify commercial opportunities from (a) reallocating existing resources, and (b) identifying insights about the 'rules of engagement' and translating these rules into business value. You could loosely summarise this as 'entrepreneurial thinking'.

Reallocation is an important source of value. Research suggests that companies that more actively reallocate investments deliver, on average, 30 per cent higher total returns to shareholders annually than companies with a more static approach. The 'entrepreneurial thinking' approach is probably easiest explained with the examples below.

Example

Shrink wrapping

- **Situation** – Potential supplier A recommends a manufacturer of consumer goods to reduce packaging costs by replacing a cardboard outer case from supplier B with a shrink-wrap alternative supplier A can provide. This requires an investment in shrink-wrapping equipment. The time to earn this investment back is less than two years, based on current annual volumes of purchased cardboard boxes and the cost difference for the supply of shrink-wrap film required instead.

- **OBC action** – OBC analysis identified that a 25 per cent reduction in cardboard cost is required for a break-even NPV on the shrink-wrapping investment. At this level, the manufacturer would be financially indifferent about the chosen solution, assuming all other things to be equal. Having historically achieved low single-digit price reductions for these outer cases in annual sourcing initiatives, the manufacturer shares this insight with supplier B. The manufacturer explains that he intends to use shrink film going forward and cease the purchase of outer cases on the grounds of a compelling price difference.

- **Outcome** – Supplier B offers a 20 per cent reduction in price. The reason for doing so is explained by the fact that losing a substantial volume would cause supplier B higher fixed costs on his remaining volume. The supplier does pose a condition: the price is to be revisited in case the supplier can replace the volume with better priced volume to another customer. The manufacturer accepted the 20 per cent price reduction in favour of making the wrapper investment. Although the price reduction was not sufficient to achieve an NPV break-even situation, it vastly reduced the returns on the shrink-wrapping investment and practically deprioritised the project.

- **Bonus** – Subsequent industry experiences showed this happened to be a fortunate decision. Shrink-wrapped products turned out to stack poorly and cause increased hidden costs in manufacturing and retail customer supply chains from requiring more floor space and from product falling over.

Example - bag in a box

- **Situation** – A long-standing manufacturer produces a liquid food ingredient and sells this in returnable stainless steel tanks. The marketing department is considering a change in product packaging to a *Bag-in-Box* (BiB) offering. This follows an increase in competitors using this packaging format. The change will require an investment to refit dispensing equipment installed at the customer base.

  There are no particular complaints about the stainless steel containers. Although the marketing manager is concerned about being at a competitive disadvantage, there are no hard data or trends to suggest that the business is missing sales opportunities by not offering its product in BiB. There is some commercial flexibility in the size of the BiB product, which comes in four sizes compared to, essentially, one for the steel containers. Yet, the lead BiB product (2.5 gallons) is close to the size of the steel container (3 gallons).

- **OBC action** – Revisiting business profit drivers unveiled a ~200-year payback period (!) for the dispenser refitting investment. In addition, an unutilised shelf-life advantage was uncovered for steel tanks over BiB, particularly in the small customer segment. The shelf-life advantage means that some customers would not be able to use the full contents of a BiB pack before its contents expire. Using a steel tank would allow them to reduce the amount of product they would have to throw away.

  The increase in packaging costs for BiB would roughly be offset by savings in logistics from better stacking of the product on pallets in warehouses and on trucks. The annual cost for the steel tanks (mainly cleaning) is very low. The tanks are capital items with an economic life of 10 years. Due to very little wear and tear, tanks are used well beyond this point (the average container life is over 15 years), with no annual replacements of the tank fleet to speak of. From a production standpoint, the business has the capability to supply in either format.

- **Outcome** – The review made the business realise that BiB technology had been an enabler for new entrants to access the market, with a lower fixed and higher variable cost compared to steel tanks. In addition, any customer with tank-fitted equipment would not be able to operate a BiB product without a costly dispenser refit. This provided an additional barrier for customers to switch to BiB – and, to most competitors.

Based on the OBC, the marketing team revisited its commercial strategy, capitalising on the shelf-life advantage. The new strategy increased prices on low volumes to reflect the value of the longer shelf life compared to BiB. It also clarified that the business would not actively promote BiB, and provided clear, profit-driven criteria for accepting BiB volumes. In essence BiB volumes would only be accepted if there was a real concern that the business would miss out on a profitable customer.

This approach removed a long-standing distraction from the corporate agenda, improved the profitability of an unattractive segment and avoided the need for costly (and non-value adding) mid-life equipment refits to the tune of $12m.

What these examples show is that insights derived from the OBC analysis can deliver substantial economic value to an existing set-up. Yet, this value could *only* be discovered by looking at the situation through the lens of a new opportunity. In neither of the examples would the benefits have been uncovered by merely looking to optimise existing processes.

Try this

- Identify all parameters where your solutions could possibly be different from one another.

- Determine at what point on the scale one alternative trumps the other, and why.

- Use a holistic approach to identify sources of value. Just because a difference between alternatives does not have any value for *your business*, this does not mean that it does not have any value for anyone up- or downstream in the value chain. Keeping cardboard volume on the production line had value for the cardboard supplier. Not having to discard expired product had value for some stainless steel tank customers.

- Find a way to make the other party aware of this value, and you are probably close to finding a way to claim your share of that value.

- Don't take anything for granted. When you have an insight that changes the rules of the game, existing assumptions, for example about acceptable cost reductions or price increases, may need to be thrown overboard in order to open the door to your share of the benefit.

Tips

- When developing the OBC, remember to review findings and insights on their potential to be utilised, even if you decided not to pursue the opportunity.

- Use the think-outside-the-box tips from Section 2.3 to identify areas to probe.

What would you really, really do without money?

Reflection

- How did it work?

[ ]

- What will I do next time?

[ ]

Reference

Hall S, Lovallo D and Musters R (2012) How to put your money where your strategy is. *McKinsey Quarterly*, March 2012. See www .mckinsey.com

Chapter 4

Ensure your decision is the right one

4.1 Align with company strategy

No matter how great the idea, the last thing you want to do is to spend time on something that is just not right for the company. Resources are scarce and every company has its own role to play. Activities outside the company's strategic arena are a potential distraction in terms of resource allocation and management attention. This largely translates into hidden costs elsewhere in the business. Therefore, have clarity on the agreed strategic priorities for your company, and play only in that space.

Alignment with strategy is no excuse for not making any money. Always be clear on how your initiative gives the company a stronger competitive position, whether from a profit-generating or enabling perspective.

Source: Paul Vasarhelyi/Shutterstock

Do this
Play to your strengths. Stick with things your company does best.

4.2 Validate your Right to Succeed

Working on the right problem is one thing. Making it a success is another. Management's role is to ensure a balance between risk and return when it comes to resource allocation. How confident can they be that this project is worth its salt? Even if you have all your ducks in a row internally for a successful implementation, have you thought about how competitors may respond? More poignant still, if there are others jumping at the same opportunity at the same time, what determines who comes out on top? And where does your business stand in that picture?

Source: Everett Collection/Shutterstock

Do this

Identify the factors that entitle you to be successful at delivering the outcome. Are there any Achilles' heels you know about?

4.3 Avoid the 'there is no doubt' decision trap

Decisions in business are often driven by urgency. So if there is no doubt about the case for investment, why should we spend any time analysing our Right to Succeed and other value drivers? On that thrust, people are often unwilling to raise an objection on something where they may not have a ready alternative to hand, especially when it appears clear that something must be done anyway.

If there ever was a sure sign to spot ill-considered decisions, it has got to be the 'there is no doubt' cohort of red flags: often easy to disprove and capable of saving you from throwing money down the drain. Be ahead of the game and spell out your own no-doubts before someone else does. An eye-opening exercise in humility and honesty!

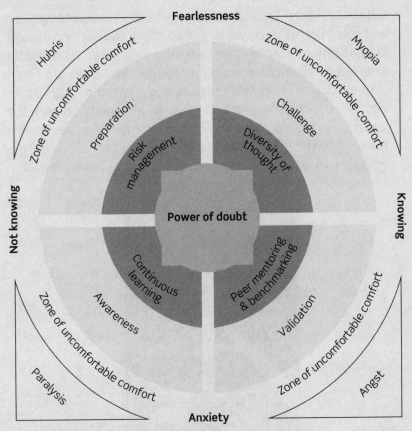

Source: from The CEO Report, *Embracing the Paradoxes of Leadership and the Power of Doubt*, Heidrick & Struggles, January 2015

Do this

Stop, think and ask. Is the project being pursued for the right reasons? Why? All of it? Now? (Hint: the justification is the useful part of the answer.)

Reference

The CEO Report (2015) *Embracing the Paradoxes of Leadership and the Power of Doubt* Saïd Business School and Heidrick & Struggles, January 2015.

4.4 Ensure early vertical alignment

Especially in larger organisations, projects are developed by a team and served up for approval by stakeholders and decision makers at head office when the team is ready to go. Often there is little time left for review, let alone for changes. Reviewers are faced with a dilemma. They feel pressured to respond quickly to prevent the business missing a key window of opportunity. Yet, the projects are typically complex and often contain surprises or gaps that must be addressed. Without taking corrective action now, the project is likely to cause business issues further down the line.

Source: Amma Ewa Bieniek/Shutterstock

Do this

Identify stakeholders higher up in the organisation and seek their advice early on in the process. This way, their views and concerns can be taken into account in crafting the project business case.

4.5 Don't second-guess your leader

Leaders are sometimes baffled about the proposals that come their way under the flag of 'This is what you wanted.' Often taken as a well-intentioned prompt, occasionally as a blank cheque, leaders' statements about priorities for the organisation are easily interpreted as 'This is something I care about and will regard favourably when it comes to allocating resources.'

Source: CrackerClips Stock Media/Shutterstock

Rearing its head across the array of business proposals, this is especially likely to surface in proposals that are otherwise thin on substantiation, often because there isn't enough to justify them.

Leader's response: 'Be prudent. Do what makes business sense. Leave me out of it.'

Enough said.

Do this

Expect your leader to assess every business case with the same degree of rigour and integrity. Prepare your proposals accordingly.

4.6 Be clear about what you are giving up

Disappointing financial results of projects originate from two main sources: optimism and ignorance. What you are giving up is particularly easy to ignore. And why wouldn't you? It's not causing much objection and most of the time you aren't using it anyway.

It's often much later that questions will arise about avenues that have been closed off. Take this into account in your project assessment to get a more complete picture of your project and where it adds value. Awareness of what you are giving up increases the sense of responsibility to deliver the value from what you are doing instead.

Can you see what that does to the credibility of your project?

Source: gualtiero/Shutterstock

Do this

Identify what the organisation is giving up beyond money to bring the proposed initiative to fruition. Are any bridges being burned?

4.7 How does this fit with other things going on?

Just about every project is more complex than we initially imagine it to be. When we have finally mapped the critical path and all dependencies, we feel that we're ready to tackle the project head-on.

If everything were only that simple.

Source: 123rf.com

Projects themselves often depend on other projects being completed on time. Where they don't, they are likely to influence a piece of yet another project. Of more immediate concern is that resources needed for a project are often constrained. Sure, budgets are one thing. But they are relatively easy to address. The bigger issue – and a potentially large hidden results driver – is formed by the people and tools designated to contribute to a project. Typically, they are not standing by, waiting for the project to start. Most of the time, they will be involved in other projects and the demands for their contribution will exceed their available hours.

Get the picture? Paint it ahead of time. A few well-placed strokes can make for a different landscape.

Do this

Make it a routine from the beginning to ask everyone involved about the dependencies they see for the project and keep a running log as you craft the business case.

4.1 Align with company strategy

Why

Ignoring luck, sustainably successful businesses have two things in common. They are clear about their strategy and they stay focused on it.

Why does this make such a difference?

There are many fish in the sea. If we'd chase after every red herring that crossed our path, we'd never get far. The reason is that resources are limited and opportunities abound. To make the most of the cards we were dealt, we have to play to our strength. Every time we chase an opportunity that does not allow us to play to our strength, we're most likely denying ourselves to work on opportunities that do bring out the best in us. The clearer the strategy and the goals it supports, the easier it is to say 'no' to opportunities that arise. The wider this awareness around the organisation, the better its ability to self-screen out distracting initiatives.

Source: Kamira/Shutterstock

Business briefing

The purpose of strategy is to provide an overview to what the organisation is about, where it is going and how it is planning to get there. If you will, it is a micro-distillation of what the science of economics is about for an organisation: the efficient allocation of scarce resources.

Shareholders have a choice where they invest their money. They make their choices based on the stated strategy of the company, and their assessment of the company's track record combined with the opportunities in its market place. Shareholders have a not unreasonable expectation that the company can outperform the market. Otherwise, they might just as well invest in a tracker fund. As such, the trust of shareholders puts an obligation on management to stick with the strategy.

Of course, the success of sticking to the strategy is contingent on the strategy being sound and current. The latter is important so it stays relevant. If you feel your company is missing out on great opportunities because it rejects projects due to incongruence with the strategy, get the strategy reviewed first. Only then propose new projects. It typically saves time that way.

Try this

- Be genuine in your assessment of how well the proposed project (or problem) fits with company strategy. If you find yourself having to bend interpretations or having to play with words, strategy alignment is likely questionable. If that is the case, but you experience pressure to bring the case forward anyway, be open about the strategy alignment angle. Include in your analysis how to determine prioritisation of resources to this project compared to others.

- In cases where strategy is perhaps not that clearly defined with relevance to your project, the concept of sustainable competitive advantage may help you. A competitive advantage is something, whether under your control or not, that gives you an edge over the competition where it comes to achieving profitable sales. A sustainable competitive advantage is one that is slow to erode and difficult to copy. If your project helps to build, strengthen or lengthen your sustainable competitive advantage, it ought to be in line with strategy.

- If you have already come some way to developing an idea that ends up not fitting with the company strategy, that doesn't have to be the end of the road. Consider how others can bring it to fruition, either by selling it through a joint venture or licensing arrangement of sorts.[1]

Tips

- As a litmus test, if it isn't immediately obvious to a relative outsider, say a spouse, see whether you can convincingly address their questions. If not, perhaps it wasn't meant to be.
- It is easy for biases to come into play here, or to just pay lip-service to the strategy for convenience. After all, many strategy documents look alike and it is easy to say that something strengthens your competitive position. Remember that we want to be able to look back on having taken the best decision. Does this fit the bill?

Reflection

- How did it work?

---

[1] See Section 6.5 for more on exit strategies.

Ensure your decision is the right one

- What will I do next time?

4.2 Validate your Right to Succeed

'What looks like resistance is often a lack of clarity.'
(Chip and Dan Heath in *Switch*)

Source: Pressmaster/Shutterstock

Why

Project champions often express surprise and frustration about the length of time it takes to get a decision proposal approved. Approvers' hesitation often results from a lack of confidence in the proposal. It's not that proposals are incredible, but the reasons why that confidence is deserved are often not spelled out. And, let's face it, approvers are typically busy people with better things to do than sifting through the proposal or interrogating people to get confident that they are not just looking at a good idea. They want to know whether the company can deliver the results as well. The better you can spell that out, the faster decisions will get approved.[2]

Business briefing

The 'why' is clear: you want to crystallise your Right to Succeed to establish management or investor confidence in your project. Confidence stems from credibility. Credibility in turn stems from proof. In this case, proof of probability for success.

Perhaps more important is that understanding your Right to Succeed makes you better understand the foundations of your project. It identifies the base for the project's value and pinpoints the factors that you should keep an eye on as potential destabilisers.

Try this

Here's a list of items that I have gathered over the years to validate the Right to Succeed. Regard this as a dynamic set; you may well want to add your own favourites.

Business case - is it a good idea?

- Matches company experience and expertise
- External landscape thoroughly assessed
- Stakeholders aligned
- Current position or bridgehead mandates the venture

▶

---

[2] Mind you, speed of approval should not be an objective in its own right. Yet, I typically see proposals get approved markedly faster when they are clear about their Right to Succeed.

Implementation and value delivery - can it be done?

- Implementer involved in decision making
- Resources available
- Project team aligned
- Responsibilities clear
- Targets achievable
- Costs validated
- Integrated past lessons
- Risk planning and mitigation in place
- Value delivery plan in place[3]

Tip

Find your own rights to succeed by answering these questions:

(1) If this is such a great idea, why is no one else doing it?

The best answers explain why your company is uniquely positioned to do this, for example through patents, current market position or earlier investment.

(2) If others are doing this already, what's in it for us?

Your project may well be a 'ticket to stay in the game'. If so, that's absolutely fine. Then try to propose solutions that 'up the game'.[4] Even something as simple as the replacement of a roof is a good opportunity to assess whether more value could be added by, for example, including solar panels, better insulation or even adding a floor to the building.

---

[3] See Chapter 5.

[4] See Chapter 2.

Reflection

- How did it work?

```
┌─────────────────────────────────────────────┐
│                                             │
│                                             │
│                                             │
│                                             │
│                                             │
│                                             │
└─────────────────────────────────────────────┘
```

- What will I do next time?

```
┌─────────────────────────────────────────────┐
│                                             │
│                                             │
│                                             │
│                                             │
│                                             │
└─────────────────────────────────────────────┘
```

Reference

Heath C and Heath D (2010) *Switch*. Broadway Books.

4.3 Avoid the 'there is no doubt' decision trap

> *'Without data, you're just another person with an opinion.'*
> (W. Edwards Deming, data scientist)

Why

By the time you are writing up your business case, pressure is often mounting. People are getting excited about the bits and pieces they may have picked up on the grapevine, high-level budgets have been earmarked and potential suppliers may have schedule constraints that can impact the success of the project.

The last thing you need is someone to raise any concerns about the fundamentals of the project – let alone any minor details.

The temptation to retort these with a 'there is no doubt' one-liner grows as deadlines approach. Addressing them instead with an answer takes very little time, typically improves the decision and stakeholder goodwill, and occasionally prevents you from throwing good money after bad money.

Business briefing

As a term, 'there is no doubt' was inspired by the decision-making process leading up to the invasion of Iraq by US forces in 2003. The US administration justified the invasion on the grounds that Iraq was alleged to be illegally stockpiling weapons of mass destruction (WMDs). Although no proof was found for this prior to the invasion, the term 'there is no doubt' was used repeatedly by senior political figures in press briefings and political hearings about the alleged stocks of WMDs.

There is some debate about whether or not WMDs were found in any substantial quantity to justify the war effort. It suffices here to say that expectations about WMD stocks were markedly larger than any materials subsequently discovered. The war had accumulated an estimated financial cost of USD 1.7 trillion by 2013 (and potentially growing to 6 trillion by the 2050s through benefits payment to war veterans and interest), aside from the significant human and societal costs.

From a decision analysis perspective, our interest is to contrast the magnitude of the commitment against the robustness of evidence used.[5] This is especially noteworthy as armed force interventions are notorious for their inherent absence of mid-way 'off-ramps' and have a tendency to cost more and take longer

---

[5] This book is not the place to pass judgement on the validity of any decisions. The aim of referring to actual decisions is to illustrate and to crystallise learnings for decision making at large. As we will discuss elsewhere, we aim to make the best decision based on the best insights and information available to us at that time.

than originally envisaged. The Iraq invasion was no exception with costs originally expected to amount to at least USD 100 billion for a two-year involvement.

With this knowledge in mind, it is a small step to proof our own decision-making processes by looking for tell-tail signs of a potential 'there is no doubt' mindset.

Try this

- No-doubt questions have the potential to make you feel uncomfortable, whether you are the asker or the responder. It may at times almost feel silly to raise the point. Don't let that hold you back. As a responder, the discomfort will typically come from not having the answer at your fingertips and knowing it will be difficult to produce a robust black-and-white response. Either way, discomfort is no excuse for avoiding the issue. This is what you get paid for – to raise and resolve.

- Below are some questionable statements I regularly see people use as a shortcut for 'Let's just keep moving, shall we?' On their own, none of them is good enough to justify a project. Behind each is a suggested 'Let's dig deeper' approach for removing the doubt. Look for similar statements in your own decision environment.

  - **It has already been approved.** The paperwork just needs to catch up with reality. Let's make sure that the paperwork is robust. If the 'approved' decision needs to be adjusted, it's better to show guts and step on the breaks now. (Note: Good governance is occasionally confused with red tape. Businesses with good governance would not allow a situation to exist where managers could take decisions without a vehicle to hold them to account.)

  - **The CEO wants this.** This is often an interpretation and a disguised attempt to deflect accountability. Sure, most CEOs want issues to be resolved. They trust their managers to take the right decisions to get there. Any CEO would be

▶

reluctant to sign a piece of paper that is little more than a blank cheque to 'solve what you wanted us to solve'.

- **It is a strategic imperative.** Have we proven that? Strategies that don't make any money won't get us very far. Do we understand the value created by the strategy and the role of the specific project within that?

- **We have done this many times before.** That may be true, but that doesn't mean we need to do more of it. Is this a problem we need to continue to address? If so, is this still the best solution? What have we learned from past implementations? What has changed over time and how have we adapted to that?

- **There is a burning platform.** If so, stem the bleeding. Distinguish between what must be done immediately to prevent avoidable damage, and making choices that have further-reaching strategic impact. It pays to have a nurture/hold/tolerate/release view of your activities on hand to guide your thinking for 'burning' situations.

Source: Ron Frank/Shutterstock

- **The efficiency savings alone will pay for it.** Efficiency improvements are great. When it costs money to achieve them, think twice. Many efficiency initiatives enable you to do the same activity in less time or with less effort. Unless you can use the time freed up to generate more value or actually remove costs from your cost structure, the benefits are just nice to have. Ask: How does this translate into cash savings or incremental profit?

- **It's a no-brainer.** Really? Tell me how.[6] What would stop making it a no-brainer? What would it take to get there?

- **They are begging for this solution.** That is no substitute for understanding the urgency and strategic importance of the problem, and the appropriateness of the proposed solution. Better spend your time doing your homework.

- **We cannot afford not to do this, despite poor returns.** If true, this should point to some value that is harder to pin down. This may be a strategic enabler or part of the benefits might be intangible. For both types, working with a range may be the answer here. Show what value future steps may be able to unearth from building on a strategic bridgehead, albeit possibly with additional investment. For intangibles, develop a point of view on how much value the benefit will have to the company, both at least and at most. What makes you say so?

Do these answers change the question of affordability?

Tip

The more involved we are with a company or project, the harder these 'no doubt' statements become to spot. Ask yourself what questions a spouse or child would raise about your project, or a shareholder who prefers a higher dividend over reinvestment this year. Only this time you won't get away with answering 'Just because!'

---

[6] The shrink-wrap investment in the example of Section 3.7 was initially presented as a no-brainer project. A little 'undoubting' changed that.

Reflection

- How did it work?

- What will I do next time?

References

See http://www.reuters.com/article/us-iraq-war-anniversary-idUSBRE92D0PG20130314 14 March 2013.

See http://www.cheneywatch.org/speeches-and-interviews/cheney-interviews/interview-with-vice-president-dick-cheney-nbc-meet-the-press-transcript-for-march-16-2003

4.4 Ensure early vertical alignment

Why

In most organisations, approvers complain that they get to hear about upcoming decisions too late in the day. They dislike reviewing decisions under time pressure, especially when that pressure leaves little room to challenge and change things. It is much better to be pro-active and use executive input to benefit rather than hinder the project.

Business briefing

How late executive involvement happens

We have all seen this before. An idea starts to shape in a few heads and evolves into a raw business case. Someone mentions exposing top management to an early draft to get some buy-in. Everyone agrees that this is a good thing to do. Yet somehow this moment gets pushed back time and again. The case isn't quite ready yet and no one wants to be embarrassed by a lack of answers to the potential barrage of questions about the project. The never-quite-ready dynamics of business case crafting perpetuates this situation until the business case is ready or until something forces a decision to be taken soon.

Benefits from early alignment

The most obvious benefit from early alignment is time. If sounding out an executive results in the realisation that the project is not meant to fly, the early calling off can save substantial amounts of time that can be used on more valuable projects. And when projects *are* good ideas, early alignment can help save time in the approval stages. A well-briefed executive team is more inclined to review a submission sooner since they know their views have been heard in good time and they know to expect it. Although speedy sign off should not be an objective in its own right, early sounded-out ideas tend to progress faster through an approval system for exactly this reason.

Source: Leah-Anne Thompson/Shutterstock

Beyond simply saving time, executives can also make valuable early-stage inputs based on their knowledge, experience and insights. As a result, they are then also more likely to check in on the project later on, creating an informal circle of ownership.

Try this

- Use a formal process such as a regular innovation review or project pipeline review to ensure every project moves through stages and gates. This is typically a good forum to bring senior leaders and other stakeholders up to speed early and at regular intervals.

- Ensure that relevant inputs about other projects in the pipeline are also integrated back into the business case for your project.

- Make it part of your business case crafting routine to identify at the beginning who is likely to have to approve a project. In larger or more complex organisations, not all senior approvers are likely to be part of a project pipeline review. Find a way that works for your organisation to get their inputs and concerns early on in the process.

- Use interactive sessions such as a pipeline review meeting, a bespoke call or an agenda item on a business review session to achieve vertical alignment. That way, senior leaders can hear, and build on, the questions and concerns of others. If that is not possible, try individual interactions before resorting to email.

- If you end up using email, be explicit about the questions you want specific input, guidance or support for. These may be items that have featured in discussions with others or potential deal-breakers. In your request, leave room for voluntary contributions beyond your list.

- For complex projects, you may need to check back in for alignment, perhaps more than once. Schedule this upfront, whether as a specific date or a project milestone.

Tip

When any project gets chartered, require every head of department to sign off on the charter at this stage.[7] This way, all departments will know from inception what is going on. If it does not concern them, the heads of department can just sign off and move on. If they have concerns to address, want representatives from their department to be involved, or want to stay informed of progress, this is the moment to capture that. No excuse now for saying they weren't aware!

Reflection

- How did it work?

- What will I do next time?

---

[7] Electronic applications exist in the marketplace to make this swift.

4.5 Don't second-guess your leader

Why

Favour fact over fiction. This is one of the key themes of this book. The one area where this is most conveniently overlooked is where it comes to interpreting leaders' priorities and principles. Supposed priorities are often based on remarks taken out of context, and occasionally taken as a cue for a shortcut on robust decision making. Most leaders don't want things done because they say so, but because they are right for the organisation. They expect their associates to act accordingly, rather than as proverbial puppets on a string.

Business briefing

Leaders often have full agendas and are typically perceived to be difficult to get to. Everyone scrutinises the messages leaders broadcast into the organisation, whether it is on-site visits, periodic meetings or in blogs and emails. People identify themes and draw their own conclusions from these as it relates to their work.

Especially when a leader says something specific about a theme, for example 'I think sustainable energy initiatives are the thing of the future,' employees may think that the leader will look particularly favourably at initiatives in the sustainable energy space. This can particularly spark enthusiasm for initiatives that have been on the drawing board for some time, but where the business justification has been thin on the ground. In those cases, an over-reliance on a connection with the favoured theme/geography/solution type may result in a seemingly good story, but with little evidence to justify it as a sound business decision.

Employees occasionally forget that business leaders are people just like everybody else. They have been through the mud earlier in their career and are now in a position where they have responsibilities to uphold. Although there are exceptions, most leaders will want to be able to see eye-to-eye with their board members over the integrity of any business cases they sign off. A business case that can easily be read as 'we're doing this because the CEO thinks it is important' is not something many leaders would support. And with good reason; they don't have the evidence or insight to hand to substantiate it. It would just hurt their own integrity, an asset most of them know to treasure.

Example

In his book *The Science of Success,* Charles Koch relates the anecdote where he discovered that one of his businesses was periodically creating what was known as 'charts for Charles', just because he had once out of interest asked some questions about certain aspects of the business. The business did not use the charts or any related insights otherwise. As soon as Charles realised this, he asked the business to discontinue the production of the charts. Beyond his original interest, he was first and foremost keen that the business should use its resources where they could create value. This just shows how easily leaders' remarks can be misinterpreted and lead to unwanted actions supposedly on their behalf.

Try this

- Treat every business case with the same dose of integrity.
- Spend time on analysing costs, risks and returns in relation to the magnitude of each of these.
- Do yourself a favour and identify any CEO interest, perceived or real, as early as possible.
- Validate the nature of the interest and be sure to put some markers down on expectations.
- Typical areas where expectations management is useful:

  - Certainty around cost, risk and returns (often initially determined as back-of-envelope, presented as a given and pitched too optimistically).
  - Time and resources required for a robust business case.

▶

- Driver(s) for urgency.
- Opportunity cost; for example, we can prioritise this, but only at the expense of delaying project XYZ.
- Where possible, be clear about the trade-offs that may need to be made between things such as accuracy, rigour, principles and business needs.

Tips

- If you find yourself second-guessing or if discussions recur about which way the CEO would be inclined, stop as soon as you realise this. Spend your time instead on clearly articulating the question that needs clarifying and put this in a succinct message to the leader concerned. Stick with facts, be clear about your uncertainties and be open-minded about the answer you may get back.
- Be mindful in any communication that the leader may previously have been led to have a rosy understanding of the proposed project. Therefore, a pre-amble that includes the phrases 'initial assumptions' and 'further analysis has revealed that . . .' will go a long way in setting a receptive stage for presenting your question(s).

Reflection

- How did it work?

- What will I do next time?

```

```

Reference

Koch C (2007) *The Science of Success: How Market-Based Management Built the World's Largest Private Company.* John Wiley & Sons.

4.6 Be clear about what you are giving up

Why

It's often only later that we realise what bridges we have burned by choosing to use a resource in a particular way. The clearer you are about the resources you need and the trade-offs involving them, the better you can crystallise the opportunity cost. The clearer that picture, the lower the probability of regrets and surprises.[8]

Business briefing

Spectrum

The opportunity cost of resources varies depending on the extent to which their potential use is already defined. On the one extreme we find money, for which the type and timing of use are still completely open. On the other end we find resources for which the type of use is highly defined by their location, capacity, capability and availability. The question is less about *how* the resource is used and more about *whether* it is used at all.

---

[8] This only refers to regrets and surprises that relate to the use and value of resources. There is still plenty of opportunity for surprises to emerge on other fronts.

Money

Opportunity cost is often thought about in monetary terms – probably because of the word 'cost'. With money, you can make choices about whether to spend it on a car, education or a house, to name a few examples. However, once you have made your choice and spent the money on a car, you may not have enough money left to make a down payment on a house. Then the opportunity cost of spending the money on the car is not being able to buy the house you want and you may need to continue your current living arrangements longer than you intended to.

Source: vladm/Shutterstock

When it comes to opportunity cost, the great thing about money is that if you don't know how, whether or when to use it, you can just park it in the bank and use the money later. The only potential opportunity cost of parking money in the bank is that you forego higher returns from opportunities that you don't know about, don't have the appetite for or don't have the non-financial resources for to seize them anyway. Since you wouldn't have taken the opportunities for any of those reasons, that opportunity cost can be considered irrelevant.

Time

At the opposite end of the spectrum is time. With time, it is a different story. Time cannot be stored for later use. Now it's here and now it's gone. Neither can you take a 'time loan'.[9] In an organisational context, the opportunity cost of time is often embodied by how the available hours of the workforce and production equipment are spent.

The implication of time's momentary utility is that to maximise your opportunity (or to keep your opportunity cost low), you must be in a constant endeavour to work on your most important initiative.[10] The two things you cannot afford are (1) too many activity switches for ever better opportunities, and (2) too many distractions from your most important venture, even if those distractions are just exercises in evaluating your opportunity cost to yet another new initiative.

Source: iQoncept/Shutterstock

The question is then how to keep focused on your most important opportunity in the confidence that you are not passing up even better opportunities. This comes down to doing your homework upfront. Be clear about the objective you want to achieve in the grand scale of things and the milestones that need to be reached for that. Those milestones are typically reached by completing

---

9   Although time is finite and momentarily perishable, a body of literature has emerged in recent years addressing the question of how to free up time, either by improving in-house efficiency, making explicit choices about what *not* to do or by using any form of outsourcing.

10 No wonder that the Optimised Base Case originates from the discipline of operations management.

a project or a collection of projects. Once this is clear, all your energy can be put into achieving those milestones. Should a new opportunity come along, you know you will only be interested in hearing about it if it helps you achieve your next milestone faster, better or both. Anything else can just be ignored. The freedom and focus this creates are of enormous value in getting things done.

Enabling resources

Enabling resources are a group of resources for which the use is yet to be determined. The more choices we make, the more avenues of opportunity we close off. Some are closed off indefinitely, whereas others can be reopened at the expense of a switching cost or by reversing developments completed.[11] A 'greenfield' piece of land is a great example. Initially, the range of opportunities for use is only limited by imagination. Examples can vary from mining and excavation to use as landing strips or for transport, residential, commercial and industrial applications. But once some broad choices have been made, for example to construct a building, this will restrict the possibility to use the land as an airfield or for mining activities. Below is an example of where the future use is already pretty well defined.

Example – opportunity cost of land

Two manufacturing sites of the same business are located about 50 miles apart. Site A is a modern, state-of-the-art (SOTA), highly efficient plant on the outskirts of a thriving city. The plant is about 10 years old.

Last year, the business was lagging behind on its capital spending and decided to use part of the capital budget instead

---

[11] A great analogy, that goes well beyond the scope of this book, is known as Waddington's epigenetic landscape, succinctly described in Nessa Carey's book *The Epigenetics Revolution*. The model explains the fate of a cell in development by comparing it to a ball rolling down a hilly landscape with troughs en-route complicating potential changes and reversals to the course of cell development.

for the purchase of a piece of land. The plot was adjacent to site A and its owner was looking to sell quickly. The business obtained the land for £10m, about 10 per cent below market value according to experts. The site is situated well for transport connections and suitable for general industrial activity. There is continuous demand for land in industrial zones in the area.

Site B is a 40-year-old site that has outgrown its footprint. Material flows on the site are illogical, some of its infrastructure causes employee health concerns and there is no room for expansion. Over the years, the site has become surrounded by residential properties and there is the opportunity to sell the site for £20m to developers. To continue operating on the site would cost a minimum of £4m (for worker safety compliance), without any incremental benefits to show for it.

A project team proposes to sell site B, expand plant A onto the recently bought land and relocate site B's operation to site A at a cost of £18m. This will use approximately half of the recently bought land. The operational efficiency gain will roughly offset the increased shipping costs to the customer base currently served from site B.

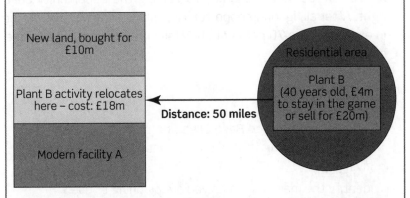

The proposal shows no charge to the relocation project for the cost of the land used on site A. The team's justification for this is that the business owns the land already and the business will not see a reduction in its cash balance by the project utilising the land. No matter how reasonable, by using part of the land for the project, that land cannot be sold anymore on the real estate market or used for other opportunities. Therefore, a charge for the land should be taken into account for the project. The opportunity cost is not just a paper cost, it is a real cost that the business would also have to incur if it had relocated operation B elsewhere. By using the land, the cost is incurred by having less land left to sell – and therefore easily overlooked.

The next question then is *how high* the charge for the used land should be. As a starting point, the average square foot price is fine. However, do think this through. If your use of the land affects the marketability of the remaining plot, this needs to be reflected in the charge. Examples could be that the transfer of operation B will affect accessibility to the site or the availability of utilities such as power and water. How desirable is it to have B as a neighbour? It may not be possible to nail this down with precision, but any real estate agent should be able to give a rough assessment on the extent to which the expansion of site A will have an impact on the value of the remaining plot.

As you can see from this example, the thinking through of the impact of your choices is key to getting the opportunity cost right. After all, ignoring opportunity costs is an important factor in explaining the 70 per cent shortfall in returns for the average capital project.

Try this

- Define the Optimised Base Case first so that you know that you are comparing to the most valuable alternative you are giving up.[12]
- Identify the main resources you are planning to use.
- Distinguish between implementation ('putting the project in place'; use often temporary) and execution ('earning the money back'; duration of use defined by the project).

---

[12] See Section 3.1.

- For resources currently in use, compare their usage value to their usage value in the project. Are any other projects considering using the resource?

- For idle resources, understand the reason that the business has retained these and compare that to the cost or value of releasing them. Are there any alternative uses?

- For resources acquired for the project, how does the cost of acquiring them compare to the value of other things you could do with the money?[13] Are you prioritising the highest value use of your money?

- Where applicable, include resale, upgrade or salvage value in your comparison.

- Distinguish between cash and non-cash costs.

- When challenged about including non-cash opportunity costs, use the land example (above) to explain.

- Litmus test: Do the project's benefits still justify the cost when the opportunity costs are included?

Tip

New product introductions often overlook cannibalisation as an opportunity cost. A new product is introduced and some existing customers shift their demand away from a current product. The reduction of current product sales needs to be taken into account as a cost of the new product introduction. Otherwise you would be overstating your profits in the business case. As a rule of thumb, use your fair market share as an assumption for

▶

---

[13] Typically businesses default here to using weighted average cost of capital (WACC) as a benchmark. Anything that delivers more value than the cost of funding is considered worthwhile doing. If your particular project is known to increase the WACC, use the marginal cost of capital – the cost of funding specific to your project.

cannibalised volume.[14] Do you have any insights to adjust this, up or down?

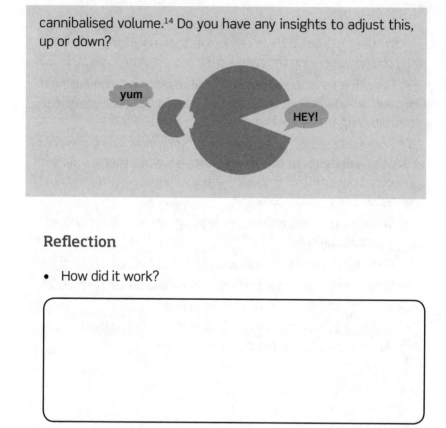

Reflection

- How did it work?

- What will I do next time?

---

[14] In this example, if you have a 30% market share, assume that 30% of your new product sales will be cannibalising sales of your existing product.

References

Allen D (2001) *Getting Things Done: The Art of Stress-Free Produc-tivity.* Penguin.

Carey N (2012) *The Epigenetics Revolution: How Modern Biology is Rewriting Our Understanding of Genetics, Disease and Inheri-tance.* Columbia University Press.

Ferriss T (2007) *The 4-Hour Workweek.* Crown Publishing Group.

4.7 How does this fit with other things going on?

'Fools ignore complexity. Pragmatists suffer it. Some can avoid it. Geniuses remove it.'

(Alan Perlis, computer scientist and first recipient of the Turing Award)

Why

Most project decisions are taken in isolation. Yet in the real world, projects are connected to other projects, either through dependency or by having an impact on them. Or both! For the business, these connections must be clear to ascertain whether something that looks great in isolation will also fit in its future operating context.

Business briefing

Complexity grows with the size of the organisation. In bigger organisations, more initiatives happen that not everyone may be aware of. As a result, surprises happen. Sometimes these are eas-ily addressed, especially when spotted early on. At other times this will require greater cost, or may even result in abandoning an initiative altogether.

Example

At the request of a local business unit, the central engineering team of a manufacturing conglomerate develops a proposal for the installation of a state-of-the-art $15m production line that should last the business a good 20–30 years. The proposal

►

includes using some empty space in a local factory. The factory is well located, right in the middle of the main volume opportunity area.

With the production line ordered, the project team starts to prepare installation and requests details about the building's existing utility supply points and capacities from the real estate team. In the ensuing discussion, it emerges that the real estate team is planning to dismantle the building within the next five years due to rising maintenance costs and mounting safety concerns. The project team needs to revisit the proposal and ends up including a charge of $3m for new building. Although initially unforeseen, the cost of having to re-house the new line within the foreseeable future, alongside potential business continuity risk, was assessed to be greater than $3m.

Source: Gunnar Pippel/Shutterstock

The good news is that in most businesses complexity is organised, akin to planetary orbits. In other words, it's more a question of them being out of sight. Once you go looking for things, there's a good chance you can find and model them quickly. Contrast this to the disorganised complexity of gas molecules' movements in a container.

Try this

- **The easy bit:** identify what your project depends on to be in place. If already in place, is its future availability guaranteed?

If not, how can we be sure it will be ready on time and in the state that we anticipate it will be?

- **The harder bit:** what are the implications of the project on current operations? Spend some time with a team with representatives from business departments to think this through. Distinguish between implementation (disruption is a likely candidate) and the ordinary course of business after implementation.

- **The hard bit:** what types of initiatives, whether already in the pipeline or not, could rely on the outcomes (= (business) results) or outputs (= things done) from this project? Does the project allow for any flexibility to accommodate that? Is that worth it? If those future projects are too uncertain, or if the cost of building in flexibility is too high in relation to the uncertainty, consciously choose to ignore them.

Tip

Make it a routine from the beginning to ask everyone involved about the three types of dependencies they see for the project and capture them as a running log as you craft the business case.

Reflection

- How did it work?

Ensure your decision is the right one

- What will I do next time?

Chapter 5

Prepare for success

5.1 Be clear about what really drives value

Assumptions and ever so slightly varying interpretations about a project's purpose[1] and its value drivers contribute to disruptive misalignments. In many business cases, volume is seen as a key value driver. Yet, most of the time volume is just the outcome of how the underlying value drivers have been orchestrated. Set yourself up for success by getting clarity about value drivers. Peel a few layers off the onion if you have to. This gives you a productive platform for efficient allocation of both resources and focus.

Source: cloki/Shutterstock

Do this

Start with the end in mind: a pound rolls into the company's coffers. What boxes need to be ticked for that to happen?

---

[1] See Section 1.5.

5.2 Prepare to be wrong

The one thing you can be sure about in your business case is that the expected returns figure will be different from actual results. Odds are it will be significantly lower. Beat the system and stack the odds in your favour by anticipating what could go wrong, either up or down.

'It's easier to do a job right than to explain why you didn't.'

(Martin Van Buren, 8th US President)

Source: Stephen VanHorn/Shutterstock

Do this

Imagine Warren Buffett is investing in your project. He has only one rule: 'Don't make any mistakes.'

What is the first thing you want to tweak in your project plan?

5.3 Work with a Range of Outcomes

It's a sobering realisation when it emerges that your expected case is counting on the sun, the moon and the stars all to shine at the same time. How likely is such a 'perfect storm' scenario? You'd think it's more often the exception than the rule.

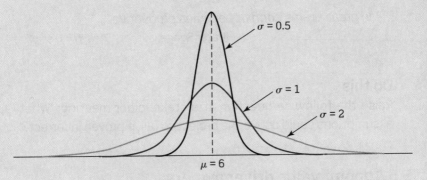

'*Just because an outcome is the most likely doesn't mean that it's likely.*'

(Harry Enten at fivethirtyeight.com)

Get real. Accept your perfect-storm scenario as an exception. Use your identified value drivers to develop a Range of Outcomes relevant to your project. Are you concerned this will shrink the expected returns? So be it. What do you think this will do to your credibility?

Do this
Imagine doing the same project ten times simultaneously (akin to a race or throwing ten dice). Although the business case is the same, the results will vary. What happens in the best case? And the worst? Why?

5.4 Encourage constructive challenge

The quest for unbiased decisions is endless. The more challenges to assumptions and rationale you encounter, the more silo-thinking is removed and the more robust your case becomes.

The one benefit offered by organised challenging is to unveil implicit assumptions. There for all to see, but rarely noticed by anyone. Taking them into account can make all the difference.

'In great teams conflict becomes productive.'

(Peter Senge, author, *The Fifth Discipline*)

Do this

Raise the following question at a stakeholder meeting: 'What assumptions could cause the project to fail, if proven incorrect?'

5.5 Appoint value driver owners

Value drivers without an appointed owner will suffer from a variety of the tragedy of the commons[2] – everyone thinks someone else is taking care of it. As a result, no one does. When crafting the business case, assign ownership to value drivers as soon as you have identified them. Clarity about ownership reduces the occurrence of things falling between the cracks.

Source: David Kochermans/Shutterstock

With their name to it, owners have an interest to spell out – and validate – the assumptions that underpin the delivery of the goods. With this validated knowledge, resource allocation becomes less of a guessing game, value delivery much more of a charted course.

---

[2] The tragedy of the commons is a term, probably coined originally by William Forster Lloyd and later used by Garrett Hardin, to denote a situation where individuals acting independently and rationally according to their own self-interest behave contrary to the best interest of all users by depleting some common resource.

Do this

Aim high: task value driver owners to develop plans that are so robust that they are willing to bet their retirement fund or child's college fund on them.

5.6 Cast the net of outcomes wide

Imagine trawling for fish with a net too narrow for the average shoal. You'll either miss part of the catch, if not bypassing it altogether. Working with a Range of Outcomes is no different. Setting the Range wide enough is key to catching the bulk of potential outcomes. It turns out humans are naturally far too confident to set the Range wide enough for catching 90 per cent of potential outcomes – a 'naturally human' net is very likely to catch only about 30 per cent of potential outcomes. Apply a few simple insights to 'right-size' your net.

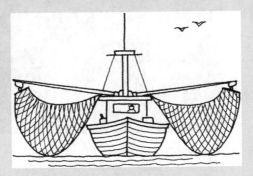

Source: Pearson Education, Inc.

Do this

Use the *highest 'high'* and the *lowest 'low'* values from a group of four to five persons as the starting point for a wide enough Range of Outcomes.

5.7 Reduce the downside, maximise the upside

It's all fine and dandy to have a Range of Outcomes that is right about 90 per cent of the time, but what good is that really going to do? Simple, really – just like with a fishing net of the right size: put it to use and use it well. You should expect three different kinds of 'catches':

1. clarity about relevant[3] potential negative return areas and how to deal with them;

2. direction for whether to focus project resources on minimising the downside or maximising the upside;

3. a 'three-dimensional' (3-D) comparison to other projects, giving a practical risk-based view on project prioritisation, particularly handy for situations where you need to prioritise projects that all appear to have the same level of returns.

Source: Greg Epperson/Shutterstock

Do this

Leverage your Range of Outcomes to determine which side of the Range to prioritise your value optimisation efforts.

---

[3] This is in contrast to sensitivity analyses, where the projected outcomes are often the result of theoretical changes to a value driver. An arbitrary value driver change of 10–20 per cent up or down is not uncommon in a sensitivity analysis, but tells little about the probability of occurrence or whether it is wide enough for the project.

5.1 Be clear about what really drives value

> 'Not everything that counts can be counted, and not everything that counts can be counted.'
>
> (William Bruce Cameron, *Informal Sociology*, 1963)

Why

Like it or not, besides getting a project approved (Is that right? No. Is it real? Yes), a lot of focus in the business case crafting process is typically on ensuring the successful implementation of a project (putting the project in place). Unfortunately, that emphasises only one side of the project coin – the cost side. When it comes to achieving the project's returns, the value delivery part typically only starts after implementation – and ought to be the more valuable and more complex half of the story. After all, placing orders and putting things together as specified is often comparatively easier than extracting sufficient value from them for the foreseeable future.[4]

Business briefing

This is where our insight into root causes comes in handy.[5] We want to be sure that we focus our attention on the causes, not the symptoms.

---

[4] This is a bit [sic] of a shortcut – no disrespect to project delivery professionals is intended.

[5] See Section 1.2.

Example

A consumer goods business is considering opening a new route to market by installing vending machines in high traffic areas. An initial review of value drivers yields a result of one: volume. The reason: there's no project value without volume. When challenged, the team applies a version of the 5 Whys. They realise very quickly that volume is a result of other factors playing their role. In this case, location, maintenance and product availability were identified as key value drivers to make this project a success.

If you think about it, that makes a lot of sense. Put vending machines in locations where few people pass and it would be difficult to achieve any substantial volumes. With vending machines essentially being unsupervised, regular maintenance checks are key. Any equipment jam would prevent the product from being sold, no matter how many interested buyers pass by every day. And without any product to sell, not many sales will be made. These types of drivers are easily overlooked because it is not so straightforward to capture them in a spread sheet model about project returns.

As vending machines embodied a new route to market for the business, the project team realised they needed to learn how to address these fairly obvious value drivers without that becoming a major distraction for the organisation. Had they not realised this, they would have relied on existing maintenance and product supply processes and would have faced regular and preventable 'non-sales' events. Using benchmarking enabled them to know what criteria to apply to location selection. This would help to determine the number of vending machines for vending 'sweet spots', instead of using an arbitrary round number.

Source: Jorg Castensen/Pearson Education, Ltd

We have already earlier distinguished between implementation and value delivery.[6] One of the reasons for this is that the individuals involved are likely to be different in both stages. Note from the vending machine example above that the identified volume drivers are mostly in the value delivery space. Even the location selection driver (implementation phase) has a strong value delivery component, whereas most implementation-related value drivers are more about cost.

All in all, the better you understand how the project will generate value and what the threats are to achieving that value, the easier it will be to focus on the things that matter. And if some are more significant than others, be sure which drivers to prioritise. Something that is harder to do may well be worth the effort.

Try this

- Identify the major benefits and costs of the project.
- Determine what factors cause these to materialise. We will refer to those of significance as key value drivers. Most projects would have 2–4 drivers. If you have more, try to keep those of significance to seven.

▶

---

[6] See Section 1.7.

- Appoint an owner for each key value driver. This includes key value drivers that are uncontrollable external factors.
- Capture the assumptions for each key value driver as you expect it to evolve, including your reasons for the assumptions.
- Highlight what you have learned from past similar projects such as this. How have you reflected that in the proposal?

Tip

If you cannot see the forest for the trees of potential value drivers, ask yourself what would keep you awake at night if you were responsible for the success of the project.

Reflection

- How did it work?

- What will I do next time?

5.2 Prepare to be wrong

'I don't believe in taking right decisions. I believe in taking decisions and making them right.'

(Ratan Naval Tata, former Chairman, Tata Group)

Why

No matter how good the idea, there are always going to be things you can't control or you just couldn't foresee. And waiting until you do is no good, because by then the opportunity will have vanished (Ratan Tata's point above). Risk is inherent in business decisions. The trick to success is to not bite off more than you can chew. The benefits of doing this upfront are:

1. being able to think things through in a less pressurised situation promotes creativity and potentially better solutions;

2. having the option to put safeguards in place upfront reduces risks and distraction from 'fire-fighting'.

'I have only two rules. The first one is: Don't lose. The second one is: Never forget the first rule. It really isn't so much having a lot of brilliant decisions, it's just not really having some terrible ones.'

(Warren Buffett, investor)

Business briefing

Warren Buffett optimises his chances by sticking to the industries he knows and risks he understands – what he refers to as his 'circles of confidence'. His approach is driven by the notion that fighting fires distracts from what you're really trying to achieve. The better you understand the Range of Outcomes, the better you can get prepared ahead of time.

Ratan Tata's quote can be interpreted as 'Don't over-analyse, let's get going and fix whatever comes our way as we go along.' This needs to be seen in context. He built his conglomerate starting from India. With continuous change in the market place and a slow, cumbersome judicial system, that mindset makes a lot of sense.

The notion that things will work out by fixing as you go along has been described by Albert Hirschman in 1967 as the phenomenon[7] of the 'Hiding Hand'. Inspired by Adam Smith's 'Invisible Hand', it can be summed up as the idea that when a person decides to take on a project, the ignorance of future obstacles allows the person to rationally choose to undertake the project, and once it is underway the person will creatively overcome the obstacles because it is too late to abandon the project.

Although based on inspirational anecdotes, recent research argues that there are really two hiding hands – a 'benevolent hiding hand' (Hirschman's) and a 'malevolent hiding hand' – with the latter featuring in the substantial majority of projects. This hand hides not only the initial obstacles and difficulties, but also the barriers to creativity itself. Long story short, it pays to know upfront what you're getting into.

Try this

- Let the value driver owners individually map out their worries.
- Have them review their concerns as a group and prioritise those that require addressing by 'book-ending' or mitigation.[8]
- Review the project's risk management plan with stakeholders for alignment.

Tip

Use the 'spouse test' to make sure you haven't overlooked anything.

---

[7] As distinctive from 'principle'.

[8] See Chapter 6 for in-depth tips and insights about putting a risk management plan together.

Reflection

- How did it work?

- What will I do next time?

References

Flyvbjerg B and Sunstein CR (2015) The principle of the malevolent hiding hand; or, the planning fallacy writ large (1 September 2015). *Social Research,* forthcoming. See http://ssrn.com/abstract=2654423

Forbes (2010) *Jay-Z, Buffett and Forbes on Success and Giving Back.* 23 September 2010. See www.Forbes.com

Hirschman AO, Cass RS and Alacevich M (2014, first published in 1967) *Development Projects Observed.* Brookings Institution Press.

5.3 Work with a Range of Outcomes

Why

Keeping a cool head in project decision making *and* implementation is of tremendous value for success. A Range of Outcomes gives you just that. Done well, it shows a clear picture of the interaction between key drivers, how extreme things may get, and the impact on returns. That knowledge helps you focus your energies where they matter most.

Make no mistake – the Range of Outcomes is no blank cheque to end up with returns anywhere within the identified Range. The project owner should sign up to, and be accountable for, an expected return.

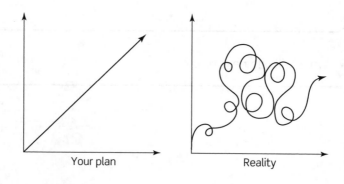

Your plan | Reality

Business briefing

I first encountered the Range of Outcomes while working for a subsidiary of Koch Industries Inc. (KII). KII's businesses are run based on Market-Based Management (MBM)®,[9] a set of principles the company credits for its over 2000-fold growth since 1967.

The Range of Outcomes is probably best described as a 'framed sensitivity analysis'. The issue with sensitivity analyses is that they are frequently used as an indicator for the robustness of a project. However, the changes used for the input factors tend to be arbitrary percentages. Although it is somewhat useful to understand how much your sales will rise or drop given a 5 per

---

[9] In his book *The Science of Success*, KII chairman Charles Koch outlines how the company translated theoretical concepts into tools for achieving superior results. Refer to Section 4.5 for bibliographical reference.

cent change in earnings, it doesn't tell you anything about the relevance of that information to your project.

As one executive puts it:

'It's very important to understand that the [Range of Outcomes] analysis is not a sensitivity analysis. It's not just saying: "If the volume grows five per cent faster, it adds one point to the IRR. If the volume grows slower, it takes a point away." That's arithmetic. The Range analysis is a real analysis of what could realistically happen on the upside that would drive positive returns, and what could realistically hurt the returns on the downside. This gives you two completely separate benefits, both of them very important.

The first benefit is that it actually helps you make decisions among projects. If you have two projects with a 21 per cent IRR, how do you decide which is better? They're both the same. But if one of them has a 50 per cent upside IRR and an 18 per cent downside and the other has a 22 per cent upside IRR and a 0 per cent downside, it becomes immediately apparent that the first project is actually better. Because the range of returns is so much better.

The second benefit is even more important. It helps you to direct the project teams to focus on eliminating or doing things they can to minimise the risks that would drive the downside, while actually trying to execute things that will enhance the likelihood of the upsides happening so that you end up with a better return in real life.'[10]

The Range of Outcomes aims to capture key value driver extremes and to translate those into the impact of those extremes on the returns of the project. With a tailored approach such as this, one key value driver may show a 5 per cent downside Range and a

---

[10] See Section 5.7.

20 per cent upside Range and another may move between a narrower Range of −5 per cent and +1 per cent. What matters is that the Ranges are:

a. value driver specific, and

b. relevant through substantiated assumptions.

Try this

- The technical analysis is going to require some serious spread sheet expertise. Ask your spread sheet expert to develop a model that is flexible so that you can use it for future projects as well. The more important work is the *thinking* behind your assumptions for the Range.

- Imagine doing the same project ten times simultaneously (akin to a race or throwing ten dice). Although the business case is the same, the results will vary. Some will be highly successful, others will disappoint.

- Assume that one out of the ten times will be an outlier event; either extraordinarily lucky or unlucky. The other nine will be captured by your Range of Outcomes.

- For each key value driver, describe what the *circumstances* look like for the most favourable version of the project. Do the same for the least favourable outcome. Use the table below as a tool to capture your thinking.

- Where possible, explain the reasoning for your outcomes. Could you have been more or less aggressive? Would that make sense for a Range that is right 90 per cent of the time?

- Review your assumptions and rationale for the upside and downside case with the stakeholders and integrate their inputs in your Range analysis.

| Key drivers | RANGE OF OUTCOMES | | | Owner |
	What can cause downside?	Assumption for expected case	What can cause upside?	

Tips

- Is your set of assumptions for the expected case nearly identical to your upside case? This may well be the result of an optimism bias. Contrast both cases and challenge the distance you would expect between them.

- To get started with assumptions, be creative. Look at things such as historical data, industry trends, commercial perspectives, similar project analogies and even your own gut feel.

- When describing the causes to the up/downsides, try to stay away from numbers where possible and describe in words what must happen for the scenario to occur.

- There is no reason for your expected case to be halfway between the two extremes. Some drivers simply have more upside than downside and vice versa.

Bonus tip

For each key value driver, identify the value that would yield a break-even (zero) NPV. What does its position compared to the Range tell you about the risk profile of the project?[11]

---

[11] See the Appendix for an example.

Reflection

- How did it work?

```
┌─────────────────────────────────────────────────────────┐
│                                                         │
│                                                         │
│                                                         │
│                                                         │
│                                                         │
└─────────────────────────────────────────────────────────┘
```

- What will I do next time?

```
┌─────────────────────────────────────────────────────────┐
│                                                         │
│                                                         │
│                                                         │
│                                                         │
│                                                         │
└─────────────────────────────────────────────────────────┘
```

Reference

Closed-doors interview with Jos van Rozen, March 2014.

5.4 Encourage constructive challenge

> 'The person who figures out how to harness the collective genius
> of his or her organization is going to blow the competition away.'
> (Walter Wriston, former Chairman and CEO, Citicorp)

Why

Two influential inhibitors of excellence in decision making are silo thinking and bias. Filtering these out early on has tremendous value. If you leave it to the market to do it for you, your tuition is likely to be substantially higher. Using constructive challenge is an efficient way to tap into the collective insights and knowledge residing in the organisation. Of particular benefit is the potential to challenge conventional thinking and identify implicit assumptions.

Business briefing

The underlying thought here is that the collective genius is better than that of the individual. This applies to context setting, problem identification and brainstorming for alternatives all the way through to solution development and the post-completion review.

'The greatest obstacle to discovering the shape of the earth, the continents and the oceans was not ignorance but the illusion of knowledge.'

(Daniel Boorstin, twelfth Librarian of the
United States Congress (1975–1987))

Disinterested dialogue

A literature review identified six defining elements of disinterested ('unbiased') dialogue likely to influence the effectiveness of a decision: 'evidence base, use of disconfirming information, a portfolio approach, transparency, participation of the most appropriate individuals, and careful consideration of divergent opinions.' You can probably see how using each of those elements would help establish a fact-finding culture.

'A strong decision review process is more important than analysis in producing good decisions by a factor of six'.

(Dan Lovallo and Oliver Sibony, The case for behavioral
strategy, *McKinsey Quarterly*, March 2010)

A connected study found that robust analysis alone will not naturally result in good decisions. Highly disinterested dialogue is the ingredient needed to deliver a significant rise in the return on investment on projects. Often it's the dialogue that improves the robustness of the analysis. Although good analysis is a critical ingredient for decision making, it turns out that process is more important than analysis in producing good decisions (those that actually increase revenues, profits, productivity or market share) by a factor of six. Wow, now it gets interesting!

It turns out it's often the critical review process that ferrets out poor analysis. Conversely, superb analysis is useless unless the decision process gives it a fair hearing.

Constructive challenging is also an important tool in the knowledge processes at Koch Industries. Besides sifting fact from fiction, rumour, hunch and opinion, I learned there that challenge sessions can also serve to identify implicit assumptions.

Implicit assumptions

Implicit assumptions are the things we take for granted without even articulating them. An example would be that the sun will rise again tomorrow. In this case it almost feels ridiculous to even spend time contemplating that it wouldn't rise. Yet, turning implicit assumptions explicit upfront could have made for a positively different turn of events in these examples:

Example

Costa Concordia

The rapid sinking of the *Costa Concordia* cruise liner, causing the death of 33 people off Italy's coast in 2012, baffled many. After all, along with aviation, cruise liners are one of the safest forms of transport.

To ensure cruise liners remain afloat when a leak is incurred, they have been divided into sealable compartments. Should a compartment take in water, it is evacuated and sealed off. The displacement of the remaining compartments then keeps the ship buoyant.

The compartments are sized so that buoyancy is guaranteed even if two compartments fill up with water. The implicit assumption here is that no more than two compartments will take in water in an incident. The *Costa Concordia* defied this assumption. It sailed

---

at full speed too close to a rocky coast. When it made contact with a sharp rock, its momentum caused the rock to tear the hull over 53 meters, flooding five contiguous compartments, rather than in just one place. A lesson for the shipbuilding industry is to revisit compartmentalisation.

Source: Gerasymovych Oleksandr/Shutterstock

Philae lander

After 10 years preparation and construction the Philae lander was launched in 2004 and took another 10 years (!) to travel from earth to land on a moving comet to do research and send pictures back to earth. Impressively, everything went to plan. However, 60 hours after landing in November 2014, contact was lost. It turned out that the probe had landed in a shadowy spot near a cliff face where its solar panels had insufficient exposure to sunlight to power its equipment.

Source: melowilo/Shutterstock

Implicit assumption: the probe will have sufficient exposure to sunlight to power its equipment.[12]

Are you sold on the value of crystallising implicit assumptions yet?

Black swan effect

In workshops, people often mention the 'black swan effect', as described by Nassim Taleb. This is defined as: 'a metaphor that describes an event that comes as a surprise, has a major effect, and is often inappropriately rationalised after the fact with the benefit of hindsight.' The main idea in Taleb's book is not to attempt to predict black swan events, but to build robustness against negative events that occur and be able to exploit positive ones.

Source: efirm/Shutterstock

We distinguish implicit assumptions from the black swan effect with the former being a broader category that includes non-outlier effects. When looking for implicit assumptions, the objective also is not to predict events, but to identify assumptions and their validity boundaries.

---

[12] Since then, possibly enabled by a shift in the comet's position in relation to the sun, Philae made contact with Rosetta, its comet-orbiting 'mother ship', on a few occasions in 2015. This contact revealed enough to know that most scientific equipment appeared to be undamaged, but the brevity of contact also suggested that no sufficient power was available to carry out its original scientific mission.

Example

In the energy industry, the shale oil revolution took off against a background of historically high oil prices, particularly driven by demand in developing economies. American shale oil producers have subsequently become victims of their own success. The flood of new oil supply they created has caused a collapse in the price of crude, which dropped from more than $100 per barrel in June 2013 to less than $50 in January 2014. This saw many shale oil rigs in the USA close over the same period, with shale production costs [validity boundary!] estimated between $50–70 per barrel. It should therefore not have been a surprise that Saudi Arabia as OPEC's most influential member – and with production costs of $4.50 per barrel – did not support OPEC production cuts during this period, thus sustaining a period of oversupply.[13]

Try this

- Constructive challenging ought to happen regularly throughout the business case crafting stage. For projects that get approved with significant residual uncertainty, continue this into the implementation stage.

- In their book *Collective Genius,* Linda Hill *et al.* comprehensively set out specific rules of engagement for constructive challenging:

  'Generally, the rules of engagement fall into two categories. The first is how people interact, and those rules call for mutual trust, mutual respect, and mutual influence – the belief that everyone in the community has a voice and that even the inexperienced and less tenured should be

▶

---

[13] Note that production costs do not tell the whole story. Saudi Arabia's dependency on oil is so high that in 2015 it was estimated to need an oil price of $105 per barrel to balance the country's budget, highlighting another reason to maintain high production rates.

allowed to influence decisions. The second category is how people think, and those rules call for everyone to question everything, be data-driven, and see the whole.'

- McKinsey has come up with a practical solution for screening for confirmation and optimism bias, identifying to what extent constructive challenge is still required. The sensible health warning issued with the tool is that the questions should *not* be answered by individuals who have developed the recommendation or who have driven the decision process.

Decision-making checklist

Consideration of different points of view	YES or NO
Have the recommenders checked their assumptions?	
In their analysis, have they considered factors that would make the project exceed its initial goal?	
Have they compared their assumptions with those made for a comparable external project?	
Have they compared their assumptions with those made for a comparable internal project?	
Have the recommenders integrated a diverse set of opinions?	
Have they assembled a diverse team for the decision-making process?	
Have they discussed their proposal with someone who would most certainly disagree with it?	
Have they considered at least one plausible alternative to the course of action being recommended?	
Total 'yes' answers	
Consideration of downside risk	YES or NO
Inside the organization, what are this decision's two most important side effects that might negatively affect its outcome? Have the recommenders considered these side effects?	
Side effect A	
Side effect B	

In the company's industry, what are the two most important potential changes that might negatively affect the outcome of this decision? Have the recommenders considered these changes?	
Potential industry change A	
Potential industry change B	
In the macro environment, what are the two most important potential changes that might negatively affect the outcome of this decision? Have the recommenders considered these changes?	
Potential macro-environment change A	
Potential macro-environment change B	
Total 'yes' answers	

Source: adapted from 'Are you Ready to Decide?', April 2015, *McKinsey Quarterly*. www.mckinsey.com. Copyright (c) 2015 McKinsey & Company. All rights reserved. Reprinted with permission.

Screening matrix

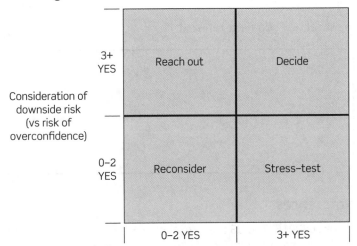

Source: adapted from 'Are you Ready to Decide?', April 2015, *McKinsey Quarterly*. www.mckinsey.com. Copyright (c) 2015 McKinsey & Company. All rights reserved. Reprinted with permission.

Tip

To identify implicit assumptions, get challenge groups to address the following question: *What assumptions could cause the project to fail, if proven incorrect?*

Reflection

- How did it work?

- What will I do next time?

References

Crooks E (2015) The US shale revolution. *FT Magazine*, 24 April 2015. (http://www.ft.com/cms/s/2/2ded7416-e930-11e4-a71a-00144feab7de.html#slide8)

Garbuio M, Lovallo D and Sibony O (2015) Evidence doesn't argue for itself: The value of disinterested dialogue in strategic decision-making. *Long Range Planning*, 48: 361–380.

Hill LA *et al.* (2014) *Collective Genius: The Art and Practice of Leading Innovation.* Harvard Business Review Press.

Krucoff C (1984) The 6 o'clock scholar. *The Washington Post,* 29 January 1984 (cited).

Lovallo D and Sibony O (2010) The case for behavioral strategy. *McKinsey Quarterly,* March 2010.

Meissner P, Sibony O and Wulf T (2015) Are you ready to decide? *McKinsey Quarterly,* April 2015.

See http://mbm.blogs.com/team_weblog/2009/03/the-challenge-process.html

Taleb NN (2007) *The Black Swan: The Impact of the Highly Improbable,* 1st edn. Penguin.

See http://www.rina.org.uk/costa_concordia_damage_stability.html

Wikipedia – Black Swan Theory. (See https://en.wikipedia.org/wiki/Black_swan_theory)

5.5 Appoint value driver owners

Why

We have talked about ownership before[14] and you may be forgiven for wondering why it resurfaces here. To make a specific point, really. Section 1.7 explains the importance of clarity about ownership for the areas of implementation (so you can tap into your reality check) and value delivery (to construct interest-driven operational engagement in implementation). However, now that we have identified our key value drivers, creating clarity about driver ownership helps to ensure value maximisation within the Range of Outcomes.

Business briefing

The main distinction in key driver ownership is between controllable and uncontrollable key drivers.

For controllable key drivers, the owner's role is to line up the right resources at the right time to deliver the expected value for his key driver. Where there's a conflict or resource constraint, it's up to the owner to identify and resolve that, or to ensure timely escalation for resolution. In addition, the owner works with the

---

[14] See Section 1.7.

implementation team to find ways to minimise the probability and impact of the downside case occurring and to do the inverse for the upside case.

Source: PzitivStudija/Shutterstock

For external key drivers, the owner's prime responsibility is to:

a. understand the key driver assumptions for the Range and their validity boundaries

b. monitor key indicators at a frequency that allows for sufficient lead time from raising an alert to putting corrective action in place

c. agree with relevant stakeholders what key indicator values should trigger a 'trip wire' to activate mitigation plans

d. develop mitigation plans for the key driver

e. where relevant, put guard rails in place to limit the impact or probability of the downside case occurring

f. use the same approach to seize as much upside as possible

g. where relevant, allocate resources as needed and include the cost of the above in the cost of the project.

With all of that in place, you can just imagine a project control room becoming a forward-looking asset in value delivery, in stark contrast to the rear-view mirror value gained from providing Gantt chart status updates.

Try this

- Appoint owners with the relevant skills and expertise.
- Ensure Range management plans for individual key drivers are joined up for a holistic approach.
- Have stakeholders constructively challenge the consolidated Range of Outcomes and the proposed actions for Range optimisation.

Tip

For high credibility, brief key driver owners that their belief in their own plans must be so robust that they are willing to bet their retirement fund or child's college fund on it.

Reflection

- How did it work?

- What will I do next time?

5.6 Cast the net of outcomes wide

Why

We all know that reality is different from the straight-line plan. We can probably overcome any of the hurdles that we encounter in isolation, but are we prepared for the whole journey of ups and downs *and* still make it to the other end? The better you understand the journey ahead, the better you can prepare for it, and the better your chances for reaching the other side.

For projects, working with Ranges does that for you. It helps you understand the potential risks and upsides to the project so that you can already begin to put things in place to minimise the downside and maximise the upside. The major fallacy here is that people predominantly work with too narrow Ranges.

Business briefing

The brain is particularly overconfident of its ability to estimate accurately. This is often illustrated with a simple quiz: guess the weight of an empty jumbo jet or the length of the River Nile. Participants are asked to offer a Range of which they feel 90 per cent confident instead of a precise figure; for example, the Nile is between 3000 and 9000 miles long. Typically, participants fall into the same trap: rather than playing safe with a wide Range, they give a narrow one and miss the right answer. It appears, unlike John Maynard Keynes, most of us prefer being precisely wrong rather than vaguely right.

Source: Binski/Shutterstock

In decision-making workshops I run, we do a similar exercise. Questions appear to be general knowledge, but are quite specific. Participants are told to set the Ranges for their answers with a 90 per cent confidence level; i.e., one wrong Range is allowed out of ten questions. The reason for 90 per cent is that we want a Range that catches most outcomes. Working with near-certain Ranges would be unproductive. It would take an enormous amount of resources and yield little value. Compare it to buying all the tickets in the lottery; you are certain you have the winning ticket, but in fact you lose out because the administrator also takes a cut – and all you get back is the money you paid out in the first place.

Source: Jcjgphotography/Shutterstock

Interestingly, despite that analogy, participants on average get correct Ranges for about 30 per cent of the questions, with different individuals getting different Ranges right. They typically do this seated around a table with three others. The exciting thing then is that when the lowest downside and the highest upside estimates for the table are taken as the Range, tables typically get 85–90 per cent of Ranges right.

Lessons

1. **We are naturally inclined to set our Ranges too narrow,** despite people admitting they have no idea of what the right answer is. The implication for a Range of Outcomes is to look for ways to widen your Range.

2. **Ranges get even narrower when we think we know the answer.** This is shown when the original questions are swapped with questions about the participants' industry (an area where they think they would know the answers). Interestingly, the percentage of right Ranges also shrinks, though with large variations.

3. **Group work works.** It only takes 4–5 people to get pretty close to a target 90 per cent Range.

Note: All this referencing to percentage confidence levels gives quite a scientific impression. Although we aim to be methodical and fact-based in our approach, setting a Range of Outcomes feels actually more of an art than a science. Every situation is different and there are highly intuitive and discussion-driven elements to the process.

Try this

- **Individual Ranges first.** Recognise that collaboration with others is required for setting the Range, but start off with collaborators each capturing their individual hunches for the Range. Not all contributors need to contribute to each key driver. Have a minimum of four contributors per key driver.

- **The collective sets the minimum.** Take the upside and downside extremities from the group as a minimum starting point for the Range. Discuss ways to stretch the Range with the contributors and cover whether outcomes could conceivably fall into the stretch area if you did the same project ten times.

- **Substantiate.** With all the focus on facts, we ought to do better than using hunches for our Range. We want to understand what influences our Range so that we can feel confident about its validity. Where possible, connect your thinking back to facts.

- **Fill in 'fact blanks'.** Where facts are not available, consider finding practical approximations. Two suggestions:

  1. Use the 'agree to disagree' approach illustrated in Section 3.5. Is there a critical value for the project in the unknown Range, for example, a value that could cause the project to fail or require adjusting course? If so, identify that value and use constructive challenge to work out whether that value would fall within the Range. If it does, further work may be required, depending on uncertainty and materiality.

  2. Look for analogies from similar problems or situations. Ask experts for historical success rates.

- **Look for caps.** Where possible, identify factors that naturally cap the Range. For example, for a production capacity expansion project, sales volume is a likely key driver. The volume opportunity in your project would be capped by the maximum capacity you are proposing to put in place. In that case, the upside case question is more one of *when* the line fills up rather than how much capacity is going to be filled. That said, your Range exploration may cause you to revisit the proposed size or type of capacity addition – a reminder that this remains a dynamic process where humility is a key attribute to have throughout.

Example

Daniel Kahneman was working with a team on developing a high-school textbook on judgement and decision making. He asked the team members to write down their estimated completion date for the book. The answers ranged between 1.5 and 2.5 years into the future. Kahneman asked a curriculum expert and dean of the School of Education how

▶

long it had taken similar groups to develop a new curriculum from scratch.

The dean answered: 40 per cent of the groups he knew about never finished writing the curriculum. Of the groups that *did* finish, *all* of them took seven to ten years. When asked, the dean estimated that Kahneman's group compared just below average to the other groups he knew of. The curriculum took eight years to write.

Caution: 'Experts are good at estimating success rates but lousy at making predictions.'

Tips

- **Double and half.** For projects where the financial results are expressed as an internal rate of return (IRR), I like to work with the following rule of thumb: aim for an upside case IRR that is *double* the IRR for the expected case, and aim for a downside case IRR that is *half* the expected case's IRR. When your Range is not quite at that level, ask what could happen to have key drivers turn out more extreme and apply that to the Range. This is by no means a guarantee that you will have a 90 per cent confidence Range when you get there, but typically it's a good stretch from where minimum Ranges start out.

- **Combine facts and insights.** Use a variety of sources to strengthen your Range. For example, for exchange rates and weather, history is a logical starting point: what are the highs and lows seen over an extensive period (10, 40 years)? But insights need to be applied to validate this. Exchange rates tend to be influenced by trade flows and politics that you may need to factor in. The validity of historical weather data may be impacted by global warming.

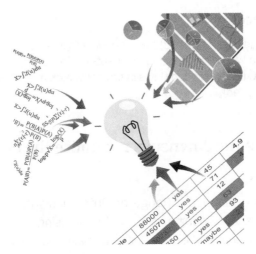

Source: mini.fini/Shutterstock

Reflection

- How did it work?

- What will I do next time?

References

Heath C and Heath D (2013) *Decisive: How to Make Better Choices in Life and Work*. Random House. Chapter 6 (adapted).

Roxburgh C (2003) Hidden flaws in strategy. *McKinsey Quarterly*, 2: 29 (adapted).

5.7 Reduce the downside, maximise the upside

Why

If you have mapped a Range of Outcomes with a 90 per cent confidence level, don't just stop at impressing executives whose approval is required. Use the Range to make the most of the project.

Viewing the project through the Range of Outcomes lens helps you understand *relevant* potential areas of positive and negative returns. Contrasting the Range of Outcomes against your expected case crystallises whether you're better off directing project resources to minimise the downside or to maximise the upside.

Business briefing

The beauty of having developed a Range of Outcomes with a high degree of confidence is that it provides you with a roadmap to delivering value. A useful Range of Outcomes not only crystallises the extent of the Range; the underlying assumptions also give clues as to how to stack the odds for success in your favour.

To do this efficiently, we distinguish between probability, impact and relevance.

Probability deals with the likelihood of a scenario occurring. It may be difficult to get an exact gauge on this, but typically you will have a sense of this by the shape of the Range of Outcomes. If you have ever taken a statistics course, you may recall the bell-shaped curve of a normal distribution, with outcomes symmetrically distributed around the expected (average) value. Most projects have an asymmetrical Range of Outcomes, either with more downside than upside or vice versa. Understanding the Range's shape is one of the key reasons for developing it. For Ranges skewed with a bigger downside Range, you may want to focus your efforts on minimising this.

Impact has to do with how much of a difference it would make. If you win the lottery, it is likely to change your life. However the chances of that happening are remote, certainly beyond a 90 per cent confidence level. In prioritising your efforts to optimise outcomes, you want to first look at factors that have both a high probability of occurring *and* a high impact if they occurred.

Example

Ice cream sales typically peak in summer months. The chances for a 'good' summer are substantial, say 1:3, but never a given. Yet in a good summer, there may be the potential to sell quadruple the ice cream sold in an average summer. However, the chances to achieve such volumes depend on the ice cream maker's ability to produce sufficient quantities and to get it to the right places fast enough. This is the type of challenge that it pays to get right.

Source: Microstock Man/ Shutterstock

High–low and low–high probability–impact combinations provide a grey area and need to be resolved through constructive challenge.

Relevance is related to context. The executive in Section 5.3 talked about two projects, both with an IRR of 21 per cent. Project A has a Range of 18–50 per cent IRR and project B has a Range of 0–22 per cent IRR. If the company's cost of capital was 10 per cent, that would be an extra reason to have to worry about the downside case of project B, since a good part of the downside case would cause the project to generate negative returns. Contrast that to project A, where the whole Range is well above negative return territory. When it comes to making choices about projects, you would rather avoid a project that looks to be a headache dossier from the very start.

If life were only that simple! If B aims to address a problem you cannot afford to ignore, this means you'll either need to go back to the drawing board, to pull out all the stops to minimise the downside case or start a strategic discussion about the business playing in that market.

Try this

- Prioritise probability–impact combinations for the key driver outcomes.
- Propose how to enhance the situation by driver through addressing probability, impact or both.
- Evaluate the cost of enhancement against the benefit. Include this in your proposal if deemed beneficial.

Tip

For some key drivers, actions to minimise the downside naturally help to maximise the upside. For others, the extremities of the Range are shaped by unconnected events. In those cases, evaluate both ends separately. Can the required actions for both ends be implemented in parallel?

Reflection

- How did it work?

- What will I do next time?

Chapter **6**

Be realistic about the risks

6.1 Know the value of risk planning

'Don't worry about whether the glass is half full or half empty. Worry about what happens when the glass breaks.'

(Attributed to Jim Collins, author of *Good to Great*)

With the average business project yielding only 30–50 per cent of its expected returns, effective risk planning is a not-to-be missed value driver. Strongly outperforming companies stay strong because they build buffers against unpredictable environments and face risk in small, steady steps. They zoom out to scan their environment for changes to risks and zoom in to assess the implications for their business plans.

Source: 123rf.com

Do this

Name your biggest project risk. What is its damage potential? What does it take to mitigate the risk?

6.2 Check for different risk types

Any in-roads made in risk management are laudable and will make a difference. But don't stop as soon as you've listed the most obvious risks. Some knowledge of risk types can help you identify a more complete set – and possibly with more important implications.

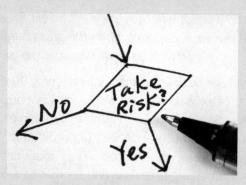

Source: JohnKawn/Shutterstock

Do this

Indicate for your top three risks how you expect to detect them. How does this affect your chances to activate effective mitigation plans?

6.3 What risks should you worry about most?

It can be intimidating to look at the world from the perspective of all the things that possibly could go wrong. Keep a cool head and separate the wheat from the chaff. When you know what needs to be done, focus on the most important risks first. In doing so, balance effort and reward. Where it gets hairy, have the composure to know when to side-step.

Risk prioritisation matrix

Probability of occurrence	1	2	3	4	5	6	7	8	9	10	
10	10	20	30	40	50	60	70	80	90	100	1st Quintile (6%)
9	9	18	27	36	45	54	63	72	81	90	
8	8	16	24	32	40	48	56	64	72	80	
7	7	14	21	28	35	42	49	56	63	70	2nd Quintile (9%)
6	6	12	18	24	30	36	42	48	54	60	
5	5	10	15	20	25	30	35	40	45	50	3rd Quintile (17%)
4	4	8	12	16	20	24	28	32	36	40	
3	3	6	9	12	15	18	21	24	27	30	4th Quintile (26%)
2	2	4	6	8	10	12	14	16	18	20	
1	1	2	3	4	5	6	7	8	9	10	5th Quintile (42%)
	1	**2**	**3**	**4**	**5**	**6**	**7**	**8**	**9**	**10**	

Low — High (Probability of occurrence)

Low   High

Potential impact

This matrix shows how the top 20 per cent of most important risks occupies a very small area and underscores the value of focusing on the (typically few) risks with the highest scores.[1]

Do this
Rate the probability and impact of each risk on a scale from 1–10. Rank the product of both scores from high to low to identify the priorities for action

---

[1] The big assumption here is that the risk scoring is accurate. The shading of quintiles is merely shown to illustrate that just scoring with High–Low indicators can leave a lot of effort spent on risks placed in the upper right quadrant that could arguably merit a Low–Low classification when looked at from a multiplied perspective.

6.4 Ask about options

This is one of the gems of risk management. Options are often the result of forethought. They're typically cheap, ready when you need them and can make a big difference by allowing you to focus on harder-to-control risks. Unfortunately we tend to be ignorant of their possibilities until it is too late. A few well-placed questions can open up a whole new world.

Source: 123rf.com

Do this

Look for potential problems in your project that can be an opportunity for a third party, should they occur. Is there a way you can structure your downside into an upside?

6.5 Explore exit strategies

Exit strategies are quite naturally associated with failure – and therefore avoided in most business cases. The paradox is that exit strategies are not best planned when failure is looming. Building them into your plan upfront can shape your thinking about project-deliverable priorities – and even tweak the scope. Understanding the different reasons for an exit helps you stratify your exit strategies by situation. Importantly, exit strategies are a key contributor to the credibility and risk profile of your business case.

Source: Robert Elias/Shutterstock

Do this

Imagine the project having to be stopped due to unforeseen circumstances. Yet your reputation comes out unscathed as you were able to recover the bulk of the invested value. How did you do that?

6.6 Set trip wires and keep an eye on things

Having contingency plans, mitigation steps and exit strategies in place is one thing. But how do you know when you need to activate them? When the ship runs aground in most cases it is way too late. Adjust course too early and you're causing unnecessary distraction and costs. This is where effective trip-wiring comes into play. Set the right ones, set them well and make sure they're connected to a bell.

Source: robodread/Shutterstock

Do this

For your top three risks, determine the lead time you ideally need to activate the best or the most cost-effective risk mitigation plan. Set your trip wires accordingly and make sure they are connected to a bell.

6.7 Erect guard rails

There are cases where a trip wire or a contingency plan just won't do. If the risk of straying off the proverbial road is unacceptable, it's time to include guard rails in your business case. Where trip wires function to raise a call for action, guard rails – in a manner of speaking – allow you to go on auto-pilot on given dimensions in the knowledge that certain risks in those dimensions have been taken care of. Although effective in managing unacceptable risks (probability, impact or both), guard rails are not for every situation; they come with a price tag and may impose limitations on project plan flexibility.

Source: hans egbers/Shutterstock

Do this

Be clear on how far you are prepared to go in accepting risks. Make a resounding here-and-no-further statement. Break the decision into smaller pieces so that you will stay within those limits at all times.

BIG PICTURE
6. Be realistic about risks

6.1 Know the value of risk planning

'Chance only favours the prepared mind.'

(Louis Pasteur (1822–1895) French microbiologist, pioneer
of the germ theory of disease, and inventor
of the process of pasteurisation)

Note: We mostly regard risk in a negative context when we assess the things that could turn out different than expected in a project. The tone in this chapter is no different. However, from the perspective of optimising value, we also explicitly want to think about what we have referred to before as upside risk. This has all to do with identifying the ingredients for the perfect storm: what happens if we look at a scenario of extremely – but likely – positive circumstances? In that case, the risk planning questions address how the project can be positioned to make the most of that positive scenario.

Why

Most car drivers have insurance because the law requires them to have it. Motoring risks are well known and therefore insurable. With projects in the sphere of enterprise, the business risk is often exactly that; something where the business will have to fend for itself. That doesn't mean you should sit back and watch things unfold. With the knowledge that the average business project yields only 30–50 per cent of its expected returns, the effort of risk planning can go a long way in securing value.

Business briefing

Effective risk planning is a not-to-be missed value driver. In their book *Great by Choice*, Jim Collins and Morten Hansen identify the traits of what they call '10x companies'. These are companies that beat their long-term industry index by at least ten times – wow, ten times! The interesting thing is that they didn't achieve this by taking high risks. Quite the opposite in fact.

Risk planning at '10x companies'

Collins and Hansen identified three dimensions of productive paranoia that 10x companies employ to stave off the effects of uncertainty:

1. **Build cash reserves and buffers against unpredictable environments.** The 10x companies didn't wait for the storm to hit. They knew it was coming . . . they just didn't know when. So they prepared carefully and methodically for its arrival.

2. **Bound risk.** The analogy for this is the 20-mile march. If you set off on a 3000-mile marching journey, you're more likely to achieve the goal when you clock up roughly the same distance every day. Doing substantially more in apparent tail-wind situations will exhaust you for subsequent days. Doing substantially less in head-wind situations doesn't exert your system enough to sustain yourself and progress on the journey. The trick is in setting a pace you can keep up.

3. **Zoom out, then zoom in.** The 10x companies possessed a 'dual-lens capability' in which they could zoom out to scan for changes in the environment and assess risk, and then zoom in to focus on the implications for their business and the superior execution of plans and objectives.

Source: Kletr/Shutterstock

They also connect this to the aspect of timing:

> 'Sometimes acting too fast increases risk. Sometimes acting too slow increases risk. The critical question is, "How much time before your risk profile changes?" Do you have seconds? Minutes? Hours? Days? Weeks? Months? Years? The primary difficulty lies not in answering the question but in having the presence of mind to ask the question.'

Risk mitigation types

Michael Herrera, a business continuity expert, defines the types of risk mitigation as follows:

> 'Risk acceptance: *Risk acceptance does not reduce any effects however it is still considered a strategy. This strategy is a common option when the cost of other risk management*

options such as avoidance or limitation may outweigh the cost of the risk itself. A company that doesn't want to spend a lot of money on avoiding risks that do not have a high possibility of occurring will use the risk acceptance strategy.

Risk avoidance: *Risk avoidance is the opposite of risk acceptance. It is the action that avoids any exposure to the risk whatsoever. Risk avoidance is usually the most expensive of all risk mitigation options.*

Risk limitation: *Risk limitation is the most common risk management strategy used by businesses. This strategy limits a company's exposure by taking some action. It is a strategy employing a bit of risk acceptance along with a bit of risk avoidance or an average of both. An example of risk limitation would be a company accepting that a disk drive may fail and avoiding a long period of failure by having back-ups.*

Risk transference: *Risk transference is the involvement of handing risk off to a willing third party. For example, numerous companies outsource certain operations such as customer service, payroll services, etc. This can be beneficial for a company if a transferred risk is not a core competency of that company. It can also be used so a company can focus more on their core competencies.'*

Source: Dusit/Shutterstock

Try this

- Identify the key risks to your business case, using the Range of Outcomes as a starting point.
- Determine their danger/benefit potential for your project.
- Work out what it takes (and costs) to mitigate the risk.
- Set your own 20-mile march target on project progress.
- Build project-relevant buffers against unpredictable environments.

Tip

In setting your own 20-mile march target, be unperturbed by what others are doing. Assess the environment and your team's abilities. Set your target to what is challenging, but does not have the potential to destruct the structural fabric of the team and its resources.

Reflection

- How did it work?

- What will I do next time?

[empty box]

References

Collins J and Hansen MT (2011) *Great by Choice: Uncertainty, Chaos and Luck – Why Some Thrive Despite Them All.* Random House, October 2011.
See http://www.mha-it.com/2013/05/four-types-of-risk-mitigation/

6.2 Check for different risk types

Why

Not all risks are created equal. Some are controllable, some not. Some matter, others don't. Some are highly probable; others akin to winning the lottery. Checking for different risk types may help you identify risks you might otherwise overlook. And understanding the types of risk you are dealing with helps you to put them into perspective so that you can best direct your time, attention and resources.

Business briefing

When we check for risk types, what we really do is to look at the different dimensions of risk in relation to our project. The resulting project-specific combination of dimensions then translates into a risk type. The list below is by no means exhaustive, but can serve as a platform from which to develop further risk insights.

Frequency

How often is there a window of opportunity for the risk to occur? Is this regular, erratic or the equivalent of a once-in-a-lifetime opportunity?

Timing

During what phases of the project does the risk pose the biggest threat to the project? Do we have a view on the evolution of the risk occurring over this time window?

Intensity

If a risk event occurs, is it an all-or-nothing occurrence (binary)[2] or can it occur in gradations? To what extent can different gradations be predicted? And what types of response or preparation are required for the various gradation levels? Do we understand where the tipping points for these 'response zones' lie?

Duration

Does the duration of a risk event matter? If yes, how long is the risk event likely to last? What is the range of duration outcomes? How should our response vary depending on the duration? More importantly, how do we know whether we're in it for the long haul? And what are the possibilities for corrective action?

Recurrence

Can a risk event occur more than once? Does that make a difference for how we prepare for it?

Impact

If the uncalibrated impact of a risk event is significant, that makes the risk a serious candidate for the risk planning short list.

Probability

Risk is often associated with probability. Probability can be addressed from a few different angles. As a starting point, it is typically useful to understand the probability that a risk occurs. But that in itself may not be that meaningful. To give meaning

---

[2] For many, a resonating example of a binary event – but not necessarily a risk – is pregnancy; either you are or you aren't. You cannot be a little bit pregnant.

to probability insights, you need to ask meaningful questions. One way to do that is to tie them to the Range of Outcomes.[3] An example would be to ask what the probability is that a key driver, say, GDP growth, moves within a band where the project yields positive returns.

Keep in mind that probabilities can give a false sense of comfort. If you decide that a risk is not worth the worry on account of low probabilities, you'd probably feel frustrated if that risk materialised anyway. For me, the role of probability is confined to gaining an *initial* understanding of priorities.[4]

Dependencies

We typically review risk only from the immediate impact it can have. But are there perhaps also second-order impacts worth considering, either on the project or on the larger business?

Detectability

Risk mitigation is often hampered by warning signs arriving late or not being recognised in the first place. A compelling example is the Indian Ocean tsunami of 2004.

Example

Over 230,000 people were left dead or missing as a result of the unannounced flood waves that reverberated around the Indian Ocean following the third-largest earthquake ever recorded on a seismograph. The short time between the typical initial retreat of the sea (clearly detectable with the human eye) and the subsequent flood wave was not sufficient lead time or warning[5] for many inhabitants and tourists around the Indian Ocean coastline to escape its devastating effects.

---

[3] See Section 5.3.
[4] See Section 6.3.
[5] Many did not know to recognise the retreat as a sign of a tsunami.

Since then, a UN-sponsored tsunami warning system for the Indian Ocean has been set up, allowing warning messages of seismic events to be sent to the 28 countries that ring the Indian Ocean within two minutes.

For risks difficult to detect, the roles of controllability and ability to mitigate will increase in importance when assuring project success.

Controllability

This has everything to do with your ability to control the *occurrence* of a risk event. An example of this is the risk of employee strikes. Most strikes are caused by disagreements over working conditions and remuneration. In large part, these are within the control of the employer and it is up to the employer to create the conditions that set the stage for an engaged and committed workforce to make projects a success. By contrast, you would typically regard the weather or other natural occurrences as beyond-control risk factors.

Ability to mitigate

Should a risk occur, you would want to be able to optimise the situation for your project, whether this is the minimisation of a downside risk or the maximisation of an upside risk. The ability to mitigate is not just answering the question of whether something can be done, but also a question of what that would take in terms of resources. And with resources, there's typically a question about the opportunity cost[6] of using them.

Try this

- Take the risks you have identified and assess them against these lense types. Does this change your perception about some risk factors?

▶

---

[6] See Section 4.6.

Be realistic about the risks

- To boost your chances of identifying relevant risks, turn things upside down and now screen through each of the risk-type lenses. Ask whether the lens brings up any risks thus far overlooked. Are you getting paranoid already?
- Use these insights to refine your overview of identified risks *and* your set of mitigation actions from Section 6.1.

Tip

Keep the process light. Put the risk types in a simple score sheet, leaving room for brief texts. Quickly review them with stakeholders for inputs, ideally in a group setting. The key focus themes will start to emerge fairly soon.

Reflection

- How did it work?

- What will I do next time?

6.3 What risks should you worry about most?

Why

Risks typically come in multitudes. The challenge is to address the ones that matter most. Worrying about getting it right is a distractor. And distraction destroys productive focus. Instead, replace erratic worry by targeted actions on the biggest risks. Working on a short list of risk factors in the knowledge that these are the most important ones to get right allows the team to apply their mental energies on doing so without having to check all the time whether there are any others that also need addressing. That confidence is created from working with a systematic assessment methodology.

Business briefing

At the core, this is very much a prioritisation game. At the very top are probability and impact as risk type drivers. For a prioritisation shortcut, score every risk on probability and impact, say on a scale from 1–10. Multiply those scores and rank the risks on the basis of the resulting product. The risks with the highest product are the ones you would want to address first.

That may be easier said than done. You may well come across risks where there's very little to address. In those cases, it is particularly important to assess to what extent the project can withstand the risk occurring and whether it is prudent to go ahead at all.

And of course we take for granted here that the probability and impact scores are reliable enough. Both are likely to have an element of estimate built in and, just to keep you humble, you may want to assess how wrong you can afford to be on these metrics.

In cases where you can afford to spend some more time, review a wider set from the risk type drivers in Section 6.2. This allows you to get a more comprehensive overview of what *must* be done and what *can* be done. The intersection of both then helps to distil the key priorities for meaningful action. Here it's helpful to remember the 'thinking outside the box' technique.[7]

---

[7] See Section 2.3.

Being imaginative about what can be done can make a difference. Using the tsunami example of Section 6.2, if something isn't detectable, that doesn't mean it cannot be *made* detectable. The challenge is then to begin with the end in mind. That may sometimes lead to initiatives that outgrow the original project. In its own right, that is no reason not to pursue it. In such a case, the risk management initiative may need to be addressed as a separate project benefiting the business at large. And depending on the potential probability–impact rating, you may even decide to put the original project on hold until the risk management element, if critical, has been put in place.

The point of doing this assessment is not to blindly follow a scoring methodology, but to develop a rationale that you can credibly substantiate and believe in. Ultimately, that forms the platform for confidence in your risk prioritisation.

Try this

- Use the risk prioritisation matrix to get a first indication of risk management priorities (**meaningful risks**).

- Review your Right to Believe[8] the credibility of the risk ratings. Acknowledge any uncertainties and take them into account in your assessment.

- Create a new matrix, mapping the risk mitigation actions in terms of priority and mitigation impact (as opposed to risk event impact). This becomes your map of **meaningful actions**.

---

[8] A Right to Believe is derived by crystallising the strength of evidence of an argument based on (in decreasing order of strength) the relevant facts, scientific proof, structured assessments, rationale, indications, assumptions and assertions used to build the argument.

Tip

Some risks may not score a high meaningful rating, but they may have a high 'noise' factor in the organisation. If that noise has the potential to distract the project team's focus from what matters, it pays to name these risk factors up front. Spell out that you acknowledge this risk and your reasons for regarding it have little impact on the project. Very obvious examples are pending leadership changes or take-over bids that could potentially impact business strategy.

Source: auremar/Shutterstock

Reflection

- How did it work?

- What will I do next time?

6.4 Ask about options

Why

Options are the equivalent of putting an umbrella in your bag when you leave the house. You don't have to use it, but you'll be glad to have it with you, should it start to rain. In most cases, options are cheap, making them akin to a self-structured, though admittedly narrow-scoped, insurance policy. And that's exactly what we're craving when we're looking to manage risk.

Business briefing

Mostly known from a share trading environment, options are perfectly suitable for managing any type of situation, provided you have a counter party willing to give you the option. As with alternatives, a little imagination can go a long way in crafting options that support your project.

Given skill, imagination and time, you can make options as sophisticated as you wish, but these elements are the foundation of any option:

- the risk and what the project needs to see addressed
- the situation in which you want to be able to activate the option
- the price of the option (contrast this against what you are willing to pay)

- what exercising the option will give you
- the extent to which the option addresses the concern, and
- the time window and potential other factors that drive the validity of the option.

Example

A landowner-farmer was looking to retire and offered his land to the adjacent factory. The factory's management was interested in buying the land to accommodate future expansion plans. However, they had little interest in spending money on the land and leaving it unused for at least the next five years (opportunity cost at work![9]). They also didn't think the owner would find it easy to attract other interested parties.

Solution: management expressed their interest and asked the landowner to give them the preferential right to buy the land should he receive a serious offer from a third party. This was documented and signed. No money changed hands! Both parties had the peace of mind that they ultimately would be getting what they were looking to achieve.

Try this

- To create an option, first of all be clear about what you want. This is the moment where it pays to think outside the box; you can only get what you're asking for.
- Clearly articulate the need in terms of what you need 'covered', for how long and what the circumstances are where you could activate the option.
- Where you need to make an agreement with a counter party, do your homework for the price negotiation:
  - Assess the value that the option would have for you. What damages, effort or lost income would you be able to avoid?

▶

---

[9] See Section 4.6.

- What value does the opportunity offer to the counter party? Is this exciting enough to offer the option to you for free? What costs, if any, do they have to incur upfront to be able to make the commitment embedded in the option?
- Document your thinking so that, should a risk event occur, there's no need for second guessing. Where engaging with a counter party, clearly document the conditions in a contract.

Reflection

- How did it work?

- What will I do next time?

6.5 Explore exit strategies

'Never walk into a room without knowing how you're going to get out.'

(CIA manual)

Why

Exit strategies provide a way out. They limit potential losses, or maximise revenue when the project has served its purpose. An option for some, a deliberate objective for others, using an exit strategy is one way to provide a book-end to your project: here and no further. Exit strategies are best planned upfront. By doing so, you know when to activate your exit strategy and you can work out whether you need to incorporate elements in your project plan to facilitate the exit strategy.

Business briefing

At the core, an exit strategy is an option when it comes to project implementation. It's a scenario that you can activate when the project circumstances call for it, but ordinarily you don't have to. However, for professional investors such as venture capitalists, the 'exit' is an inseparable part of the whole proposition; they typically invest in an opportunity because they want to sell it off to another party after the successful completion of a transformative phase of sorts. If venture capitalists don't see a credible path to an exit, they are unlikely to jump on board in the first place. For them, clarity about the exit is crucial. If successful investors take the exit strategy so seriously, why shouldn't we do the same?

Source: Pincasso/Shutterstock

Exit strategies are quite naturally associated with project failure – and therefore avoided in most business cases. The paradox is that exit strategies are not best planned when failure is looming. Building them into your plan upfront can shape your thinking about project deliverable priorities – and even tweak the scope. Understanding the different reasons for an exit helps you stratify your exit strategies by situation. Importantly, exit strategies are a key contributor to the credibility and risk profile of your business case.

Types of exit

Broadly, we can distinguish three different types of exit: targeted, unavoidable and risk management.

Targeted

The targeted exit is typical for professional investors. They may love the opportunity, but don't want to be stuck with the investment for the rest of their lives. Within five to ten years from investing, they want to be able to sell it on, having doubled or tripled their money in the process. For this type of exit, potential investors want to understand the range of choice they may have to sell the investment on to. This may include other professional investors, an existing industry player (competitor) or, in some cases, a listing on a stock exchange. The wider the range of alternatives, the more chances for an exit there are. However, to arrange those chances in your favour, it pays to have an understanding of the needs of the groups of potentially-next-to-be owners.

Unavoidable

Some projects have a limited economic life and will need to be closed down at some point in the (far) future. Nuclear power plants and paper machines are typical examples where the life of the equipment will at some point simply expire. Construction permits for these may have been issued on the condition that the site will be cleaned up at the end of the project life. Often this will include a detailed description of the expected state of the site after the clean-up, as well as instructions about how to dispose of any waste. Having a clear sense of the scope and magnitude of the exit can play a defining role in determining the overall attractiveness of a project.

Joint ventures are a special type of project and sit somewhere between targeted and unavoidable when it comes to exit strategies. Joint ventures are typically put together to combine complementary strengths of the respective partners in order to seize an opportunity that neither would be able to seize on their own with the same chances of success. Sooner or later, the opportunity may dry up or the venture may mature to a stage where the partnership nature is holding it back rather than propelling it forward.

The typical joint venture agreement will include clauses for terminating the partnership. Where the venture cannot be sold to other investors, whether through an initial public offering (IPO), management buyout (MBO) or corporate sale, the termination clauses will dictate who ends up owning the venture, sometimes using pretty draconian procedures such as Russian roulette, the Texas shoot-out and the Dutch auction. Each of these embodies a variation on how the buyer is nominated and the venture is valued. With the value of a going concern incorporating a substantial part of the returns on the initial investment, it pays to be clear and in alignment upfront not just on how the proceeds are going to be divvied up, but also on the order of preference in which the terminal value is going to be realised.

Risk management

If a project doesn't quite go the way it was envisaged, you may have to decide to take your losses and stop the project. It is easy for defeatism to take over and just scrap whatever work has been done so far. However, not all may be lost. It is always worth considering whether the outputs or outcomes of the project would have value to another party, whether internally or externally.

Containing risk exposure

Especially for riskier projects, having an exit strategy can help contain the risk exposure. Management and stakeholders are much more likely to support an initiative where potential remnants can get a new lease of life elsewhere in the business, thus minimising the money potentially at risk.

Example

A manufacturing company is considering expanding into a developing market by establishing a production plant there. Current growth rates are high, albeit off a small base, but the future is uncertain. Investing in the market now may give the business a first-mover advantage when the market really takes off in meaningful volume terms. Some managers favour continuing the current export model until the market matures, others advocate making a strategic investment to create a competitive position and secure the market ahead of other players.

The company also operates in a number of developed markets where it has had production plants for a long period. A number of those plants will require investment over the coming years to expand or replace existing production capacity. If the investment is made in the new market and fails, will there be any funding left to support the investment needs of the existing operations?

The decision is made a lot easier with the realisation that most of the equipment required by the new location can also be used in the mature market production sites, should the operation in the developed market fail. Now, the risk is limited to the money spent on project fees, land and buildings, the latter two of which may possibly be resold locally. In this context, management feels confident that, although there is a significant investment to be made, the money at risk is limited to project-specific costs and potential losses on assets sold in case of termination. Given the potential prize of becoming a leading player in a promising market, that has now become a risk the company can afford to take.

From this example it is clear that a little thinking ahead goes a long way in creating value from exit strategies. With the potential redeployment in other plants in mind, the equipment may be specified upfront so that it can be more easily adjusted to the needs of the redeployment location. Making those adjustments – think about things such as electricity standards, safety regulations or connecting to other equipment – can quickly cause costs to equal those of buying new equipment if not thought out upfront.

Try this

- Assess the project for natural exit points. Major decision moments and completion milestones are obvious candidates alongside risk events.
- Identify the value the project may have at each stage for:
  1. other parts of the business,
  2. redeployment by third parties in some shape or form, or
  3. scrap value.
- Check for exit-enhancing factors you may want to include in your business case so that it is easier to activate the business case when needed.

Source: EdBockStock/Shutterstock

Tip

Use a brainstorm session to identify the value at potential exit points. There may be more value in an ailing project than you imagine at first.[10]

---

[10] See Section 2.5.

Reflection

- How did it work?

- What will I do next time?

6.6 Set trip wires and keep an eye on things

Why

Risk mitigation and contingency plans tend to be written from a knee-jerk perspective: 'If things fall apart, this is what we'll do.' Although helpful, this is a reactive approach that may cause some preventable damage to occur. With timely alerts in place, plans can be activated earlier. This can make the difference between being able to activate *damage-prevention* plans instead of *damage-control* plans (compare using an umbrella to stay dry vs having to use a towel to dry off after getting caught out by rain).

> '*Planning without action is futile. Action without planning is fatal.*'
>
> (Unknown, http://quotationsbook.com/quote/30535)

Business briefing

Whether you are looking to timely adjust course or limit actual damage, setting effective trip wires requires an understanding of the nature of the risk and the potential responses. The nature of the risk typically defines the detectability[11] of early warning signs. The potential responses define the amount of lead time needed for a risk response to be effective. To use the umbrella analogy, if you have an umbrella to hand, your trip wire for pulling out the umbrella can be the first rain drop hitting your head. However, if you forgot to take an umbrella along and want to use one when needed, your lead time is defined by how long it takes to get your hands on an alternative umbrella. Failing that, you may have to revert to forms of damage control (phone your next appointment to inform them that you will be delayed) or accept getting wet.

'Because day-to-day change is gradual, even imperceptible, it's hard to know when to jump. Tripwires tell you when to jump. Tripwires don't guarantee you will make the right decisions. But they at least ensure that we are aware it's time to make a decision.'

Beware of the water melon

From a project management perspective, it's worth adding a word of warning about project progress reports. One technique used in progress reports is a traffic light system of red–yellow–green to indicate the extent to which things are on track. Intended to highlight focus areas for concern or action, these systems can sometimes give rise to 'false negatives' with the occurrence of 'water melons' (green on the outside, red on the inside). This is more likely in systems where the colour of the status indication is left to the respondents' interpretation and their desire to raise an alarm.

---

[11] See Section 6.2.

Be realistic about the risks

Source: Valentyn Volkov/Shutterstock

Try this

- Begin with the end in mind. Determine the need for and value of having a trip wire (regardless of knowing whether it is possible to have one). Does having a trip wire enable you to have better chances at more successful or cheaper risk mitigation? Is the achievable warning lead time sufficient for an effective response?

- Identify data sources for the trip wire. Where needed, use brainstorming techniques to identify alternative ways to trigger the trip wire.

- In most cases, the trigger for the trip wire will be a piece of information. Connect the data source to the trip wire. If this cannot be automated, appoint a risk owner who has responsibility for monitoring the trend or situation, *and* for raising the risk response activation flag.

- If data feeds are not real-time and self-feeding, determine the required frequency of monitoring to enable a timely response.

- Ensure the trip wire triggers the risk response. Road-test the mechanics of the trip wire if needed. Is it fail-safe?

- Schedule trip wire reviews as appropriate to ensure validity, fitness for purpose and potential to optimise.

Reflection

- How did it work?

- What will I do next time?

Reference

Heath C and Heath D (2013) *Decisive: How to Make Better Choices in Life and Work*. Random House. Chapter 11.

6.7 Erect guard rails

Why

There are situations where you cannot afford or are not willing to get it wrong. That's where guard rails come in. Although they may not necessarily be able to prevent a risk event or the damage caused by it, at the very minimum, guard rails will result in a less severe outcome than without them in place.

Business briefing

Guard rails come in various guises, ranging from low-cost options to significant project cost drivers. They replace uncertainty by a known, but not necessarily risk-eliminating, level of certainty. The defining identifier is that they are in place in any case and that they limit the magnitude or scope of potential damage. As a result, the project team can focus on managing other risks and value drivers.

Insurance policy – The insurance company takes over your risk. Not unlike an option, it is there when you need it, assuming the activation conditions have been well defined. At the same time, there is no obligation to use the policy. Insurance policies may include minimum claim levels ('excess clauses'), maximum claim values or a limit on claim frequencies. These may cause you to decide to 'take the hit' instead of making a claim. Use a policy too often and you may find your insurance premiums go up. Rely on it even more and you may get black-listed.

Source: zimmytws/Shutterstock

Safety net – Trapeze artists work with a safety net. It gives them and their families the confidence that they can do their work and return home safely. It also wouldn't be an unreasonable minimum requirement for a life insurance policy for trapeze artists. At the same time, the safety net should not be relied on intensively. After all, most artists ending up in the safety net too frequently are not exactly crowd pullers.

Source: 123rf.com

Controlled release – For situations where material insights are expected to be gained over the course of the project, milestones are identified to assess the risk profile in light of the insights gained. If satisfactory, further funding or resources are released. If not, the project may be called off and an exit strategy may be activated. The potential money at risk is known upfront and deemed affordable.

Back-up – Back-ups enable you to continue as normal with little or no interruption, despite the occurrence of a risk event. Airlines typically fly with two pilots when most of the time it takes just one to fly the plane. Should one pilot fall ill during the flight, the other one can take over. A policy on eating different in-flight meals could boost the reliability of this approach!

Source: Tatiana Popova/Shutterrstock

Safety factor – Safety factors aim to eliminate doubt to a very large degree, if not entirely. You've pulled out all the stops to make sure your numbers stack up. But what if you're wrong?

Is there a risk that you may get sued? Or does the potential damage generously exceed the money invested in the project? Consider ways to build in a buffer factor. Depending on your confidence, the cost of a buffer and the potential implications of getting it wrong, the buffer may vary from a percentage to a multiple.

Example

In the data industry, companies providing data back-up services typically store multiple back-ups in multiple locations, all of which can be accessed through multiple access routes. The cost of data storage and access routes is relatively cheap compared to the cost of losing a single customer's back-up even once – the reputational damage alone could seriously harm the existence of any data back-up provider and even dent the industry at large.

'It is only by being bold that you get anywhere. If you are a risk-taker, then the art is to protect the downside.'

(Richard Branson, founder, Virgin Group)

Example

Richard Branson: 'When I was 15 and wanted to leave school to start a national Student magazine, I remember [my father] telling me that I couldn't do so until I had sold £4,000 worth of advertising to cover the printing and paper costs of the first edition of the magazine, so we knew the sales would be all upside. I worked out of the phone box with even more determination to try to get advertisers to support us. Once I'd got the advertising sold I went to see the headmaster and told him I was leaving school. He told me I would either go to prison or become a millionaire! While it was a big risk to leave school, I knew I had a good idea and knew I had the downside covered, so I was confident I was making the right decision.'

Try this

- From your overview of meaningful risks,[12] identify the ones you cannot afford to encounter, whether in the implementation or value delivery stage.

- Using your understanding of the types of guard rails, develop alternatives[13] for potential guard rails and work out the costs and implications of putting them in place. Include an assessment of implications on the project itself, for example in terms of affordability, resource constraints, timing or quality.

- Evaluate the alternative guard rails and include the implications of deploying any recommended guard rails in the project's business case.

- Where the inclusion of guard rails materially deteriorates the financial returns of a project, review the potential for:

  a. enhanced project value,

  b. leveraging the guard rail beyond the scope of the project, or

  c. reclassifying potential minimum requirements for financial returns in light of the project's lowered risk profile.

- Expose the proposed guard rails to constructive challenging to help ensure a robust set of risk-reduction measures.

Tip

You know the biggest project risk you wish to eliminate. Task someone to short-list alternatives for achieving that, either in full or in part.

---

[12] See Section 6.3.
[13] See Chapter 2.

Reflection

- How did it work?

- What will I do next time?

Reference

See https://www.linkedin.com/pulse/20140224234637-204068115-
best-advice-protect-the-downside

Chapter **7**

Look back to look ahead

7.1 Understand why hardly anyone ever looks back

Just about every self-respecting organisation has a policy requiring project owners to review or audit major initiatives on costs, implementation and results. At best, lip service is being paid to this, and even then mostly on an incidental basis rather than as a matter of course.

It's rare for anyone to find any meaningful glory in performing project reviews. Where reviews are called 'audit', there's anecdotally even less appetite to contribute to the information-gathering. A little knowledge of Human Action can change that.

Source: Sabphoto/Shutterstock

Do this

Ask project business owners what they would like to learn from past projects to make future projects better.

7.2 Look back to learn some lessons

'An organization's ability to learn, and translate that learning into action rapidly, is the ultimate competitive advantage.'
(Jack Welch, former Chairman and CEO of General Electric)

Confirming what we already know (think of things such as spending record, time to completion, and delivery of benefits) doesn't add any value. However, not distilling the lessons that can improve future projects' chances of success is like paying tuition and then not attending college. Well, if you've paid the tuition anyway, you might as well get something out of it. Change the focus of project reviews from fault-finding to identifying lessons and insights for doing things better next time. A vast unexplored area is that of improving how to set better assumptions.

Source: Ernest R. Prim/Shutterstock

Do this

Right now, identify the biggest lesson you have learned from your most recent project. How can you use this in your next project?

7.3 Make it swift, painless and valuable

The most useful reviews are those where the insights are immediately needed for an initiative. The project owner has an interest to crystallise all the knowledge and ideas to maximise the value of the project. He has identified the value drivers and key risks and understands what he needs to know to stack the chances for success in his favour.

> *'I know one thing: that I know nothing.'*
> (Attributed to Socrates, classical Greek philosopher)

Many management experts have promoted the notion of learning lessons from the past. To increase the completion rate of project reviews, remove the human mental hurdles to start them by making it swift, painless and valuable. If people can see that they are uncovering deployable, valuable insights, they will be motivated to get those insights out in the open instead of hiding them and hoping that the wind of interest will pass.

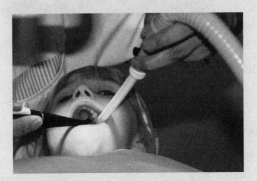

Source: Johann Helgason/Shutterstock

Do this

Schedule a short meeting face-to-face with the project owner, whether post-mortem or pre-mortem. Ask them about their proudest moments and their biggest regrets of the project. What would they do differently next time? What would they certainly do again?

7.4 Look ahead to make looking back easier

By the time that project reviews are due, quite some time has passed. People may have moved on and key lessons vanished into obscurity. Without a bespoke project review brief, reviewers are often left in the dark about where to begin and what to review. As a result, they tend to default to validating costs, time scales and benefits – the very things that are probably least interesting.

Source: Jirsak/Shutterstock

Do this

Ask project stakeholders to identify what they would like to learn from the project's review.

7.5 Have a mindset for failure

> *'Develop success from failures. Discouragement and failure are two of the surest stepping stones to success.'*
> (Dale Carnegie, American writer, developer of self-improvement courses)

For business projects, this is a company culture thing. If failure is frowned upon, no one will stick their neck out to try something drastically new or daring. Without business leaders endorsing and being seen to embrace the value of taking (controlled) risks and learning from failures, projects offering marginal improvement opportunities will be the mainstay of initiatives.

Source: Jeff Thrower/Shutterstock

Do this

In the face of a cautious corporate attitude to risk and failure, break the problem down in pieces. Aim to fail in small increments as a guard rail to risking substantial sums. Plan to learn more about the risks each step of the way for use in future projects.

7.6 Align incentives for looking back

'What gets measured gets done.'

(Tom Peters, management guru)

One of the reasons that project reviews don't get done is that employees typically don't feel the consequences of *not* completing a project review. No prizes for guessing the answer!

Source: Oleksiy Mark/Shutterstock

Do this

Establish ownership for the project review upfront. Create an incentive that emphasises the importance the organisation attaches to reviews; for example, the chance to present review conclusions and their use to the CEO or a wider group of peers.

7.7 Include lessons from the past in your proposal

'It's fine to celebrate success, but it is more important to heed the lessons of failure.'

(Bill Gates, co-founder of Microsoft, philanthropist)

It's just a matter of closing the loop, really. If you have the project review reports, why not use their findings in your proposal? The reputational damage of repeating historical mistakes can be devastating.

Source: John Foxx Collection/ Imagestate

Do this

Make it a habit to always include at least one lesson from past, similar projects in your business case.

7.1 Understand why hardly anyone ever looks back

Why

Just about every self-respecting organisation has a policy requiring project owners to review or audit major initiatives on costs, implementation and results. At best, lip service is being paid to this, and even then mostly on an incidental basis rather than as a matter of course. This means that valuable lessons are being lost and mistakes will be repeated. And that's just not right, especially because of *all* the excellence in decision-making elements we have looked at, this is *by far the easiest* to address.

£1.15 billion in 2014: the estimate value of savings and efficiency gains in public services from the work done by the UK's National Audit Office.

Business briefing

Human Action

The reasons for not performing project reviews after completion are legion. They are mostly driven by the intricacies of human behaviour. Ludwig von Mises, an economist of the Austrian School,[1] wanted to understand what causes people to do anything. He captured his findings in *Human Action.* In short, Von

---

[1] The Austrian School is a school of economic thought that is based on the concept of methodological individualism – that social phenomena result from the motivations and actions of individuals. Current-day economists working in this tradition are located in many different countries, but their work is referred to as Austrian economics.

Mises found that for humans to take action, all three of these conditions must be met simultaneously:

- be dissatisfied with the current state
- have a vision of a better state
- believe that the better state can be achieved

And if you think about it for a moment, that is not unreasonable. If you were dissatisfied with where you are, you have a dream about where you could be, but not believe you could ever get there, there's nothing that would spur you into action.

From another angle, not being happy with the current state and believing that a better state can be achieved is just synonymous with wishful thinking. Without at least a dream, if not a plan, nothing will happen.

Source: PhotoLiz/Shutterstock

People may contend you don't need to be dissatisfied with the current state and that action can be taken as a result of just having a vision of a better state and a belief that the better state can be achieved. Von Mises' response would be that people would only take action to achieve the better state if they were not completely happy with the current state – they feel they can still do better.

Getting project reviews done

So back to how we got here, project reviews are often not performed simply because no one feels called or excited to perform the review, even when it is one of their documented responsibilities. There always appear to be things to attend to that are more pressing and important than looking back at matters that cannot be changed anymore anyway. And if there is anything of interest to find, it is typically[2] about what went wrong and assigning blame for that. After all, projects that have gone well are trumpeted and show-cased so much that the apparent reasons for success are already presumed to be known. In short, it's rare for anyone to find any meaningful glory in performing project reviews. Where reviews are called 'audit', there's anecdotally even less appetite to contribute to the information gathering.

Try this

- In the spirit of Ludwig von Mises, identify high-level indicators that help you create dissatisfaction with the current state. What is your organisation's track record on spending to budget, completing on time and delivering as planned?
- Survey relevant stakeholders about their views on the utility of project reviews, what role they would like reviews to play, what lessons they would expect to learn and reasons for the current project review track record.

---

[2] See the University of Oxford study in Section 1.2.

> **Tip**
>
> The human action model is also very useful for those who are preparing a business case and want to understand whether it is ready for approval. The business case can be screened against each of the conditions from an investor's or approver's perspective to identify where further work may need to be done.

Reflection

- How did it work?

- What will I do next time?

References

von Mises L (1949) *Human Action: A Treatise on Economics*. Yale University Press.

See https://www.nao.org.uk/about-us/wp-content/uploads/sites/12/2015/12/Introduction-National-Audit-Office.pdf

7.2 Look back to learn some lessons

'An organization's ability to learn, and translate that learning into action rapidly, is the ultimate competitive advantage.'
(Jack Welch, former Chairman and CEO of General Electric)

Why

Like it or not, everything has to get better, all the time. If we don't continuously strive to improve what we do and the ways we do it, over time we will lose our relevance, whether as individuals or organisations. The market is where most of us ultimately make our living. And the market pulls no punches; if someone else is better than us, they will get the business.

'Many a false step is made by standing still.'
(Chinese proverb)

One of the most accessible, current and relevant sources for distilling lessons and insights is the collective knowledge residing in the organisation. Projects and initiatives are typically events where people are stretched, existing beliefs are challenged and adversity humbles individuals. Set away from normal routines, projects provide an inherently suitable vantage point to see what works and what doesn't. Capturing that knowledge, *and* leveraging it, makes all the difference.

Business briefing

In his book *The Fifth Discipline,* Peter Senge identifies the characteristics and benefits of the learning organisation. A learning organisation is a company that facilitates the learning of its members and continuously transforms itself. Learning organisations develop as a result of the pressures facing modern organisations and this becomes a defining feature that enables them to remain competitive in the business environment.

A learning organisation has five main features:[3]

1. Systems thinking – the way that the organisation looks at itself and its interactions with the outside world for problem solving and decision making.

2. Personal mastery – a commitment of individuals to continuous learning. Learning organisations have mechanisms to capture individual learning to the organisation's collective knowledge.

3. Mental models – these reflect the assumptions and theories held within the organisation. Learning organisations promote an open culture, based on inquiry and trust.

4. Shared vision – this creates a common identity that provides focus and energy for learning. The most successful visions build on the individual visions of the employees at all levels of the organisation. As a result, learning organisations tend to have flat, decentralised structures.

5. Team learning – this constitutes the accumulation of individual learning and improves problem solving capacities through better access to knowledge and expertise. Learning organisations tend to have great knowledge management structures, allowing creation, acquisition, dissemination and implementation of this knowledge in the organisation.

The main benefits of a learning organisation are:

- Maintaining levels of innovation and remaining competitive.
- Being better placed to respond to external pressures.
- Having the knowledge to better link resources to customer needs.
- Improving quality of outputs at all levels.
- Improving corporate image by becoming more people-oriented.
- Increasing the pace of change within the organisation.

---

[3] Fittingly going full-circle, many of these features resonate with the findings Jim Collins captured in *Good to Great* – see Section 1.3.

The point of sharing this with you is by no means that you must work in a learning organisation to draw the benefits from project reviews. Rather, the point is that consciously looking for lessons and using them has proven value both within and beyond the framework of business cases and decision making. And they're there, right in front of you. Oh, this abundance of low-hanging fruit! Anyone for seconds?

Try this

- In the spirit of 'first things first', if all you have is 15 minutes, forget about finding figures. Reserve some time with the project manager or project champion and ask them about their proudest moments and their biggest regrets of the project. Let them reflect on what they would do differently next time and what they would certainly try to do again.

Source: Mihai Simonia/Shutterstock

- Here are a few prompts:
  - What worked well?
  - What can we do better/faster next time?

- What should we look out for?
- What have we learned about setting the Range of Outcomes that should help us develop a better Range next time?
- Were there any missed opportunities in terms of getting the right people involved early enough?
- If, in the near future, the organisation is going to do more projects like the one you are reviewing, consider spending some time on doing a deep-dive exercise. Review the project from the seven lenses offered by the seven chapters of this book. You're likely to find many things that can be traced back to the business case and the related decision-making process.
- Capture the lessons and share them using communication channels that are effective in your organisation for reaching and resonating with project professionals and decision makers.

Reflection

- How did it work?

- What will I do next time?

References

Senge P (1990) *The Fifth Discipline: The Art and Practice of The Learning Organization*. Century Business.
See https://en.wikipedia.org/wiki/Learning_organization#The_Fifth_ Discipline

7.3 Make it swift, painless and valuable

Why

If you allow a little shortcut, Ludwig von Mises has shown us that people will only do things that make a positive difference and that they consider achievable. Project audits tend to take place long after the project's completion. They are complicated to perform due to (a) unclear review criteria, (b) effort required to get data, and (c) occasionally impaired credibility or relevance of available data. On top of that, most reviews have little impact and end up in a (virtual) drawer, never to be seen again. No wonder so few project reviews get completed in the first place.

Business briefing

A key inhibitor to meaningful, useful project reviews is people's preparedness to contribute. Especially where projects have gone off the rails, those involved will feel a degree of apprehension about participating in the review, unsure of how this will affect their position and future career opportunities. Without uninhibited cooperation, reviews become a sanitised version of the truth, likely containing gaps and contradictions. As a result, they have little value for improving future business cases, decisions and projects.

> *'Trust is like the air that we breathe. When it's present, nobody really notices. But when it's absent, everybody notices.'*
>
> (Warren Buffett)

Establishing trust in the review process is a key condition to achieve meaningful results. *The Speed of Trust* by Stephen

Covey is a practical resource for people looking to consciously work on increasing trust, whether for themselves, within a team or in their organisation. Suffice to say here that integrity, respect, accountability, engagement, transparency and openness are some of the key ingredients

Try this

- For relevance and value, start from the perspective of the business project owner.[4] This is the spot where the rubber hits the road: responsibility for delivering the project benefits. Identify what knowledge and insights the business project owner would want to know to enable them to increase the chances of delivering the project's benefits.

- To keep it swift, focus firstly on crystallising insights. Hold brief, semi-structured interviews with key stakeholders to identify these. Acknowledge people may feel apprehensive about getting implicated in a project's shortcomings. Show trust by assuming positive intent. Leave the finding of a supporting fact base for later, if needed.

Source: Joanchang/Shutterstock

---

[4] See Section 1.7.

- For a no-pain guarantee: be clear to your potential sources that the primary focus is on improving future decision making and project benefit delivery, not to cast judgement.[5]
- For new business cases, include a brief for the project review as an appendix to the business case. This is a great place to capture uncertainties at the business case stage to be validated for improving future business cases.

Reflection

- How did it work?

- What will I do next time?

Reference

Covey SMR (2006) *The Speed of Trust: The One Thing that Changes Everything.* Free Press.

---

[5] This defined responsibility principle is especially frequently applied in the remit of national safety boards, often active in the area of (air) traffic accident investigations. Any inputs given in these investigations cannot result in disciplinary or legal action. That independence is regarded as a critical success factor for distilling lessons for future use.

7.4 Look ahead to make looking back easier

Why

As time moves on, our perspective changes. With that, we may lose sight of the things we were uncertain about at one stage. Looking ahead at the project review serves two purposes:

1. To identify the data sources that enable a reviewer to validate the achievements and milestones of the project. Doing so upfront prevents situations where benefits cannot be validated due to lack of data. Where data sources do not exist, the project scope may need to include the creation of a tracking mechanism.

2. To define the key questions to address in the project review. Without the intent to belittle the project review effort, the exercise gets a lot easier when it can be approached from a filling-in-the-blanks perspective.

Business briefing

Transparency around the project review is a factor promoting focus on deliverables. Clarity and transparency about account-ability ensure less falls between the cracks; everyone knows what is expected and by whom. By making people aware of the lessons we're looking to learn, they will also keep their eyes open for those lessons as they unfold during the project. By having clarity about project review ownership upfront, people will know whom to approach with any observations they make that ought to be included in the review. Under such an approach, the review in a way already gets drawn up as the project progresses, rather than having to start with a blank sheet of paper six months to a year after completion. What a difference that makes!

SMART objectives

To the extent you are measuring the achievement of objectives, ensure that these are SMART. Popularised by Peter Drucker's management by objectives concept, SMART objectives were first introduced by Dr George Doran. SMART objectives are set in a methodical way so that they are easier to understand and assess on completion.

SMART objectives are:

Specific – target a specific area for improvement

Measurable – quantify or at least suggest an indicator of progress

Assignable – specify who will do it

Realistic – state what results can realistically be achieved, given available resources

Time-related – specify when the result(s) can be achieved.

It is worthwhile noting that SMART objectives don't necessarily need to be quantified. Just like our description of assumptions in the Range of Outcomes,[6] clearly qualified objectives are just as valuable.

Try this

- Ask project stakeholders what the review should cover.
- Validate whether the objectives are SMART.
- Specify where to find the data.
- If required data are not currently being tracked, include the creation of a tracking mechanism in the project scope.
- Appoint ownership for monitoring or capturing key performance data.
- Let the business project owner identify what he would ideally like to have known already (but doesn't) for the business case at hand.

▶

---

[6] See Section 5.3.

- Include an assessment of the quality of assumption-setting, developing alternatives and risk mitigation strategies as applicable. Build on this with recommendations for improvements.
- Beyond these questions, explicitly encourage the reviewer to keep an open mind about capturing any unforeseen aspects or elements that either materialised or didn't materialise.

Reflection

- How did it work?

- What will I do next time?

Reference

Doran GT (1981) There's a S.M.A.R.T. way to write management's goals and objectives. *Management Review (AMA FORUM)*, 70(11): 35–36.

7.5 Have a mindset for failure

Why

All projects carry an inherent degree of risk. Businesses go ahead with projects because, rightly or wrongly, they expect to have a reasonable chance to succeed. But not all projects do. Yet, it is in the risk taking that companies find their right to progress and sustain themselves.

'I have not failed. I've just found 10,000 ways that won't work.'

(Thomas Edison)

It is the way that companies deal with failure that sets the tone for anyone's future appetite for risky projects. Where failure is punished, people will play it safe. The trick is in the nurturing of an effective risk-taking culture where failure is regarded as part of the game, alongside the effective use of risk management strategies and experimentation techniques. Routinely reviewing progress and lessons learned – rather than upon project completion – goes hand-in-hand with embracing failure. It continuously offers opportunities to learn, adjust course and reduce risk along the way, making failure a recognised ingredient in the path to progress.

Business briefing

It's not an easy balance to get right. Business management has a responsibility not to squander the company's assets and resources. At the same time, the responsibility to shareholders also includes an element of progression, whether this is growth, re-invention or optimisation.

As the example of General Electric in Section 2.4 illustrates, many people are naturally inclined to play it safe. And who can blame them? It's only by the business being clear about risk taking being desirable that gets people out of their comfort zones. The challenge then is to foster a culture where people spend the company's money as if it was their own, and where they take risks that are assessed in the perspective of the company's ability to take on that risk without threatening its future.

Interestingly, this doesn't mean that you cannot take on riskier projects in a risk-averse organisation. You just need to play by a safer set of rules.

Soruce: 123rf.com

Try this

The following actions are intended to allow you, or your organisational environment, to embrace risk and the notion of failure in a productive way:

- Use the risk map for your project to identify how you can play it safe(r). This may mean breaking the project up in smaller pieces. It may also mean doing trials to validate some of your critical assumptions, or pilot projects to accelerate a learning-curve[7] or collect empirical data.

---

[7] A great example here is where a company is considering changing from an import model to local manufacturing. Imported products typically have a higher cost structure than locally manufactured goods. Yet, local manufacturing typically requires a certain scale before it is economically feasible. When considering a change such as this, companies often include the growth potential from being able to charge lower prices in the business case. A pilot to validate this could include the reduction of the current sales price to the sales price for a local manufacturing scenario. The company may lose money on the volumes sold while supplying the market through an import model, but gets empirical data allowing validation of the growth assumptions. Should the assumptions not be borne out by the pilot, a large investment can be halted [value!]. Should the pilot be successful, it will have created a higher volume baseline from which to start the growth trajectory, boosting the financial returns [value!].

- Be clear about what you expect to learn or achieve from each phase and how that is going to help you make a better decision about the next phase of the project. Have clear criteria for deciding on how to proceed.

- Spell out the timing implications of doing things in smaller steps. Does this cause a delay? Are there steps that can be done in parallel? Are there steps you may be able to by-pass depending on other developments? What is the opportunity cost[8] of a delayed approach?

- Develop a vision about exit strategies.[9] How much money and resources will be spent by the end of each stage and how much is potentially recoverable at various exit moments? How credible are the exit strategies in their execution potential?

- Expectations management is everything when it comes to creating latitude for failure. In your communications, be clear that you regard failure a realistic possibility, if not a necessity for learning. Mitigation plans and cut-off points are key elements to articulate and to open up to constructive challenge, where relevant.

Reflection

- How did it work?

---

[8] See Section 4.6.
[9] See Section 6.5.

- What will I do next time?

```



```

7.6 Align incentives for looking back

Why

If you are serious about crystallising lessons for the future from your projects, walk the talk when it comes to rewarding and recognising people for their contributions from reviews.

Business briefing

There are countless surveys out there showing that recognition and appreciation score higher on the list of motivating factors for work than a person's remuneration. The implication of this for project reviews is that, even if people are paid to complete reviews, they will just 'tick the boxes' if they don't find any meaning in the work itself. That is very likely to reduce the number of deployable lessons and insights to be found in reviews. In other words, incentives can play a role to help get reviews completed, but the defining difference for getting useful, relevant reviews done when needed comes from an orchestrated approach where individuals can see the immediate added value generated from performing those reviews.

Interestingly, during my time at a Koch Industries company,[10] I saw very few formal project reviews completed. At that time, a much-heard mantra was: 'You get paid when Charles [Koch] gets

---

[10] See Section 5.3.

paid.' Koch Industries reportedly reinvests around 90 per cent of its profits. The remainder is used in part to fund incentive pay for employees. This meant in practice that anyone working on a project at any stage would take an active interest in the actual delivery of the benefits from that project. Business case analysts would follow up on the credibility of original assumptions and the materialisation of risks as a project went along. For long-running projects, incentive payments could be phased over a number of years.

As you prepared for your performance review, you would identify any benefits actually delivered, lessons learned and missed opportunities. And management would take this very seriously. During the performance review window, it appeared that significant senior management time was dedicated to performance review meetings. This way, performance reviews functioned as a vehicle to both identify and deploy relevant lessons. How's that for aligning employee and ownership interests?

Try this

- Assign responsibility to every key driver owner and risk owner for distilling lessons and insights within their remit.
- Have a clear vision about the role of project reviews.
- Be transparent about how the inputs will be used.
- Have a strategy for evaluating, storing and disseminating lessons learned.
- Celebrate valuable lessons, especially from (partially) failed initiatives to ensure (a) the lessons are absorbed and (b) the value of learning lessons is emphasised.
- Consider the timing and frequency of reviews by owner. Is there any value in planning reflection windows during the project?

▶

You'll note the absence of any remunerative actions here. This is deliberate. In my opinion, if individuals don't 'get' the meaning and use of project reviews, their time is better spent elsewhere.

Reflection

- How did it work?

- What will I do next time?

7.7 Include lessons from the past in your proposal

Why

Begin as you mean to go on. If you're committed to continuous progress, start by looking at what others have learned and use this for your benefit. It underscores the value and utility of project reviews from the start and can encourage stakeholders to look for further lessons in the project at hand.

'Those who cannot remember the past are condemned to repeat it.'

(George Santayana, philosopher)

Business briefing

The very core of the Continuous Improvement Process (CIP) is the development and utilisation of feedback. This has been extensively covered in *Kaizen* by Masaaki Imai, explaining Japan's competitive success from a focus on quality and waste reduction.

When it comes to business projects and initiatives, the implication is to not just generate project reviews for the benefit of future projects. The more immediate value lies in identifying lessons learned in the past and translating those into strategies and actions for the current project.

Try this

- Look for projects like yours to learn lessons. Where possible, try to get some benefit-of-hindsight insights directly from the project business owner.

- Include relevant analogies. Widen your scope to include projects beyond the company and industry if needed.

- Disaggregate key drivers and risks. Can you find someone who has dealt with these before?

- Bring your findings back into your business case and adjust for context where needed. What strategies or actions are you proposing to include as a result of your accumulated lessons?

Reflection

- How did it work?

- What will I do next time?

Reference

Masaaki Imai (1986) *Kaizen: The Key to Japan's Competitive Success.* McGraw-Hill.

Appendix

Range of Outcomes and break-even NPV analysis:

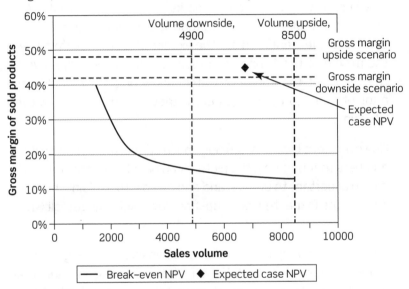

This chart depicts two key drivers; the project team would like to better understand their relationship to the Range of Outcomes. In this case they are volume (horizontal axis) and gross margin (vertical axis).

The extremities of the Range of Outcomes for both drivers are represented by dotted lines. The rectangle drawn by these dotted lines forms the Range of Outcomes between which the results are expected to fall.

Note the downside case volume appears relatively high. In this project, an existing, fully loaded production line was replaced by a bigger, more efficient line that would enable cost reductions on the existing volume and further volume growth in a growing market. Because of the existing business pre-loading the new line, the team felt comfortable they would hold on to the existing volume. The upside case volume was defined by the maximum capacity of the machine.

The diamond marks the combination of volume and gross margin that depicts the expected case.

The curved line in the chart marks the situations that would generate a break-even NPV situation. It is this line that makes this chart such pleasant reading. The expected case is comfortably in the middle of the Range of Outcomes but, furthermore, even if the team got the Range of Outcomes wrong, they would have a lot of room to be wrong before they would hit a break-even situation.

However, note that this can only make comfortable reading if the numbers that underpin the picture can be relied upon. That's why it is so important to understand and be able to explain why these data points (expected case, up- and down-side Range) fall where they do.

This is an example where the downside has largely been protected (see Section 6.7). It is worth bearing in mind that, for most projects, the break-even NPV curve is likely to run somewhere across the Range of Outcomes rectangle rather than comfortably outside it. Whilst that may make you feel nervous at first, visualising the circumstances where the project would return negative returns does two things. Firstly, it adds to the clarity and credibility of the business case. Secondly, it helps the business in aligning expectations and resource allocation for optimising project outcomes.

Index

Index